# RUBBER DUCKY
# ECONOMICS

## D.F. PAULAHA, PH.D.

PATRON BOOKS

ISBN   978-0-9723619-8-9

First published 2010 by:
Dennis F. Paulaha.

"A lot of good arguments are spoiled by some fool who knows what he is talking about."

Miguel de Unamuno
Spanish essayist, novelist, poet, playwright, and philosopher.
September 29, 1864 – December 31, 1936

# Contents

# Introduction

From 360 BC (Plato's *Republic*) until the end of World War II (John Maynard Keynes), economists had legitimate reasons to devote their time and effort to developing theories and models based on assumptions. Most important was the fact that the branch of philosophy known as economics was trying to answer important questions with virtually no data to support its arguments or conclusions.

But when World War II ended and governments around the world began collecting massive quantities of economic data, the discipline of economics had an opportunity to cut itself off from the theoretical approach of philosophy and to focus on the real economy that could now be described with numbers. The fact that economists chose (choose), instead, to remain focused on theories rather than real numbers is a major reason for political decisions and policies that lead to poor outcomes in the real economy.

Unfortunately, it is still easier, and more rewarding, for academic economists to spend their time addressing trivial questions by creating theories and models based, in virtually every case, on unrealistic assumptions.

This little book is for everyone who has to deal with the real economy.

# CHAPTER ONE

# The Questions

The first Friday in May opened with a warm spring sun that promised a new beginning. A gentle wind buffeted the still-new leaves, and as the sun moved higher in the sky, the wind picked up; not like the kite-flying breezes of April, but stronger than the mild currents that would soon mark mid-summer.

It was a day, like spring days throughout history, that raised spirits and hopes as nature once again proved that winter leads to a renewal. But, for some, that did not happen on this particular day.

David Peterson walked out of the elevator, turned right, took nine steps, and pressed his thumb against the remote entry button on his Lexus key. The lights on the big V-8 sedan flashed against the wall of the underground parking garage. Another right turn, four more steps, and his left hand found the handle on the driver's door. Then he stopped. Instead of opening the door, he stared over the roof of the black car, without focusing on anything in particular.

Thirty seconds later, he blinked; then he looked down as his hand squeezed the handle. He pulled the door open and sat down, placing both hands on the leather-covered steering wheel. Then he paused again, staring at the wall that was one foot away from the front bumper. His name was stenciled on the concrete in neat blue letters:

DAVID PETERSON, VICE PRESIDENT.

A few seconds later, he pushed the key into the ignition. As he did, he thought about the meeting he had just left. His company had to make a stop-or-go-decision on a major project, and he was responsible for determining if economic conditions were right to go forward.

He had spent the previous three months reading everything he could find about the state of the economy and talking to as many people as he could. Because of his senior position and the size of his company, he had access to top-level people in and out of government, as well as a budget that let him obtain reports from highly respected economic think tanks.

But he had a gnawing knot in his stomach as he announced at the meeting that he was certain the current economy would support the multi-million dollar investment. And it took all the nerves he could pull together to force a smile when the others had congratulated him on his outstanding presentation.

What he did not say to anyone was that he had poured over countless pieces of contradictory predictions and had listened to experts with views that were all over the board.

*And here we go*, he thought, as his thumb and forefinger tightened on the key. *It was a stop or go decision, and I said go.* He turned the key and the Lexus hummed quietly. As he pulled into the street, he thought, *I might as well have flipped a coin.*

**B**renda Jones rolled over for what seemed to be the millionth time in a night filled with demons. The demons were variations of the authors whose ideas she would be expected to use in a few hours. The leader of the pack was the professor who was giving her a 9:00 a.m. final exam on practical economics, a required course in the MBA program at her prestigious university.

Of all the courses Brenda had taken during her six years in universities—as an undergraduate and now as a graduate student—the ones that made the least sense to her were the economics classes, none of which she would have registered for if they had not been required.

But, like it or not, understand it or not, she was facing one last economics final. The problem, the thing that was keeping her awake, was that she was going to be asked to demonstrate her expertise by discussing or explaining the economics behind a number of current issues. She would have slept much better if the exam were based on material that made sense. Her only solace was that this was the last time in her entire life she would ever have to think about economics.

Or so she wanted to believe.

**K**evin and Karen Elmwood leaned back against the starboard seat of the old Pearson Ensign they had totally restored two years earlier and let the ten knot southerly wind push the twenty-two foot day sailor out into the bay.

The Elmwoods, who were in their thirties, loved sailing in May, before the heat of high summer and the still days left them becalmed for long periods of time, sometimes making it necessary to start up the small Johnson outboard hanging off the stern of the full-keel boat.

They were doing well financially, partly because they had put off having children until they felt more secure.

Normally, when they sailed, they did not talk business. Business, to them, meaning their jobs, their investments, their housing plans, and their family plans, was not part of sailing. Today was different.

Today, they were both worried about the economy—about what was happening today and what was going to happen in the future.

It was obvious to the experts in the media that the economy was not okay, but they did not know exactly what that meant. They watched television and read major newspapers and business magazines, but it was difficult to get a grip on what was happening, because it seemed impossible to find anyone who talked about the economy without having his or her pronouncements affected by his or her political affiliation.

From what they could see, there was Republican economics and Democratic economics, but no economist economics.

*No wonder they call economics the dismal science,* they thought. *Under some circumstances, the politicizing of economics and economic facts might not be a big deal; it was how the world worked. But when you are overwhelmed by uncertainty, it would be nice to have the chance to use non-partisan economic knowledge to help make the decisions and plans that could affect the rest of your life.*

# CHAPTER TWO

# Economics in the Park

At exactly 11:52 a.m. on September 27th, a medium blue 1964 Austin Mini turned off Lincoln Street and onto the narrow dirt path that led to the bandstand in the center of Jefferson Park. It was not the old Cooper S model famous for sweeping races against some of the world's most exotic automobiles; it was the basic model with only an adequate supply of horsepower and front windows that opened and closed by sliding back and forth on a track, like miniature patio doors, instead of rolling down into the door. Still, it was impossible to ignore. Not just because it was so small, but because it was pulling a trailer. Not just a trailer, but a wooden-floored flatbed trailer holding a bathtub.

The single-unit parade stopped in front of the bandstand and a man in his forties, wearing a tweed sport coat and khaki trousers, climbed out of the small vehicle. He brushed back his long, graying hair and smiled at the crowd that was gathering. After their initial surprise, the spectators noticed a sign on the side of the trailer. The sign had three words:

## Rubber Ducky Economics

There was a crowd in the park that day because of a small notice that had been placed in the newspaper. The notice read:

ECONOMICS IN THE PARK
September 27th at noon
The Bandstand in Jefferson Park

So everyone in the crowd was taken aback when the old Austin Mini pulling a trailer holding a bathtub stopped at the bandstand. They were expecting an economist, not a...whatever this was. Still, the man with the tweed sport coat looked pretty smart. And the sign on the trailer did say *Rubber Ducky Economics*...whatever that meant.

Among the spectators were Kevin and Karen Elmwood, David Peterson, and Brenda Jones.

The Elmwoods were there because they were hoping to find some help dealing with the strain on their marriage caused by not knowing how to handle economic and financial uncertainty.

David Peterson was in the crowd because he was, once again, in the middle of a stop-or-go recommendation on another expensive project and he did not trust any of the coins in his pocket to make the right decision. So, when he saw the notice in the paper, he thought he might as well have lunch in the park.

Brenda Jones was in the park because, after receiving her MBA in June, she had accepted a good, but high-pressure, job that, contrary to her hopes of a few months earlier, required her to deal with the economy on a daily basis. Although she had received an A on the economics final that had kept her awake all night, she was spending a lot of time after graduation trying to find someone or something that would give her a basic understanding of how the economy really works.

As Brenda Jones was about to discover, September 27th would be her lucky day. It would also be David Peterson's lucky day. And Kevin and Karen Elmwood's.

"Do you think we're in the right place?" Karen asked. "This isn't what I expected."

Kevin looked around at the crowd, then at the trailer with the bathtub. "I don't know," he said. "I don't know if these are the kind of people who would come to an economics in the park lecture or not. The sign on the trailer says *rubber ducky economics*, and that sounds kind of confusing."

A man in his fifties, standing next to Kevin, turned to them and said he was pretty sure they were in the right place. He was correct.

As soon as Kevin turned back to Karen, the man standing beside the trailer began speaking.

"Good afternoon," he said. "Welcome to the first ever *economics in the park* meeting. Before we begin, I want to make certain that everyone who is here belongs here."

The people in the crowd looked around at each other, wondering who might not belong.

While the people were wondering why someone might not belong, the speaker continued.

"The question each of you should ask yourself is, *Do you know why you are here*? Or, to be more accurate, *Are you willing to pay the price to be here?*

Karen leaned over and said to Kevin, "I thought this was free."

"Let me explain what I mean," the man said.

Kevin shrugged at Karen.

"If there is just one thing everyone should understand about the world," the man continued, "it is that there is no such thing as a free lunch, which means there is no such thing as a free lecture. No one had to buy a ticket to be here. And I am not going to pass a hat around. But by being here, you are giving up the opportunity to be doing something else.

And the value to you of what you are giving up to be here is a very real cost to you. Economists call it *opportunity cost*. And it is the foundation of virtually all economic thought. So take a minute to think about your options. If you do not already know why it is more important to your business life, your investing life, and your personal life to spend an hour understanding how the economy works than to be doing something else, then the cost to you of being here is too great. For everyone who does know, I want to welcome you again."

Brenda Jones knew. She knew, without a doubt, how important it was for her to understand the economy. In fact, she came prepared to record whatever transpired in the park, even though she had no idea what it would be.

And that is what she did. She recorded everything on a small, digital recorder. When she returned home, she transcribed it all. She did not use quotation marks to identify the speaker's remarks, because she wanted a clean manuscript. But she did add notes, in italics, to describe some of the action and the questions others asked.

What follows is Brenda's transcript of what the man who drove the Mini into Jefferson Park said, or, as Brenda titled it:

# Rubber Ducky Economics

# CHAPTER THREE

# Rubber Ducky Economics

*The speaker began.*

Welcome to the first-ever economics in the park meeting. Although some of you may think economics is difficult, or that it is based on some strange or secret way of thinking, it is not. Economics is pure common sense. It is, at its core, little more than pointing out and organizing the obvious.

Of course, like many things we eventually see as obvious, it often helps if someone else points it out to us first.

That is why I am here. To introduce you to a series of economic facts, which, once you hear them, should lead you to say to yourself, "I knew that."

The first fact I want to give you is that the economy is a bathtub. Well, it's not really a bathtub. But it is true that a bathtub can describe the economy. That is why I have this wonderful tub sitting on this trailer.

Anyone who truly understands the complex, elegant, mathematical models found in textbooks also knows that the purpose of such work is to advance economic theory. In the real world, however, the economy is described with real numbers, many of which revolve around the definition of Gross Domestic Product, not by elegant theories.

That is why I will be talking about the GDP economy— meaning the real economy—not a theoretical textbook economy.

It is also why I can say the economy is a bathtub.

And, when you get home, your own bathtub will be a reminder of today's discussion.

More important, anyone who understands how a bathtub works can understand how the economy works.

Now, I am not talking about all the plumbing needed

to hook up a bathtub; I am talking only about how a bathtub works.

There is a faucet and a drain. And we—hopefully—control both. We control how much water goes into the tub by opening or closing the faucet. We control how much goes out by adjusting the stopper on the drain. Of course, we do not have total control. No matter how much we open the faucet, there is a limit to how much water will flow into the tub. And no matter how much we open the drain, there is a limit to how fast the water can flow out of the tub. But, we can set the inflow from zero to some maximum flow; and we can adjust the outflow—from zero, meaning the plug is in, to some maximum outflow, depending on how much we open the drain.

Given those facts about bathtubs, we know the following. If we pick a given period of time, say thirty minutes, and we open the faucet and the drain, water will flow into the tub and water will flow out of the tub. Then, depending on whether the inflow is greater or less than the outflow, after thirty minutes, the tub will be overflowing, or empty, or it will have some water in it; the actual quantity of water in the tub being a function of the inflow relative to the outflow.

That's it. That is how a bathtub works. It is also how the economy works.

*While he was talking, the speaker connected a hose from a faucet on the side of the bandstand to a threaded pipe at the front of the bathtub on the trailer. Then he opened the faucet on the bandstand and the faucets on the bathtub so that water ran into the tub. He left the drain partially open, so while water was going into the tub, water was also flowing out, onto the ground. At this point, it was not clear if the people in the crowd thought the speaker, who was jumping on and off the trailer, were crazy, or if he were offering them something truly clever. The one thing that was clear was that everyone was saying to each other, "I knew that."*

*The speaker then put up a sign that said, "It's all about the GDP."*

Okay. Now that we know how a bathtub works, we can use that knowledge to understand how the economy works, because understanding the economy is just as simple as understanding how the quantity of water in a bathtub is determined by the inflow relative to the outflow. All we have to do is let the water in the tub represent production during some time period, a number that is normally represented by Gross Domestic Product.

Of course, the economy is more than water; it is all the things that are produced and consumed. Unfortunately, while it is easy to visualize how we can measure the quantity of water in a bathtub, if we had a giant tub filled with everything that was produced or bought during some time period, we would be looking at a giant junk pile. Well, not really a junk pile; a huge pile of good things. In any case, there is no meaningful way to measure, in physical terms, how much stuff is in the tub.

We can't add up all the things that are produced and sold during a given time period by weight or by volume, because neither measure would mean much. Or, to put it another way: As we all learned in elementary school, you can't add apples and oranges.

In other words, imagining a huge bathtub filled with all the good stuff we, as a nation, made or bought last year might be a great image, but there is no physical measure we can use to add all the Fords that were produced to all the corn that was produced to all the computers that were produced to all the apples that were produced to all the oranges that were produced and so on.

So, we add up their dollar values instead. We add up the market values of all final goods and services produced inside the country during some time period. And we call that number

**Gross Domestic Product.**

When we, meaning the government statisticians, add up all the spending numbers, they are separated into four categories: consumer spending, investment spending by business, government spending, and net exports, which are exports minus imports.

Some of you may be wondering why I am switching back and forth between two different ideas: production and spending. The answer is that when we measure spending, we are also measuring production, because whatever is bought had to be produced. You may also be wondering why the definition of Gross Domestic Product is for final goods and services. The reason is to avoid double counting; we do not want to count steel and then the cars the steel was used to produce, and so on.

There are a few other rules that are followed when calculating Gross Domestic Product.

One is that the investment spending number is for gross business investment, which means the depreciation of the nation's capital stock is ignored. If depreciation is accounted for, the final number is called Net Domestic Product, because it uses net instead of gross investment. As I said, all of this is nothing more than definitions.

Another rule is to count only goods and services that are produced inside the country. It doesn't matter if the stuff is produced by domestic or foreign companies, just as long as it is produced inside our national boundaries, which means that we exclude everything produced and sold by U.S. companies in other countries.

A third rule is that the GDP number can be adjusted to take account of inflation.

That's pretty much it. There is nothing magical about GDP; it is simply a definition. But it is a useful definition, because it offers a logical way of measuring the economy.

By following the definition of Gross Domestic Product and all the rules, we end up with a number—GDP—that is used by economists, the government, and the media to describe the state of the economy at a point in time, to compare different economic time periods or different economies, and to estimate economic growth.

So, what do we have?

Very simply, we know that Gross Domestic Product, which is a definition, is calculated by adding up four numbers:

> Consumer spending,
> Investment spending by business,
> Government spending, and
> Exports.

And subtracting one number:

> Imports.

And that's it.

*Someone in the crowd asked, "What do you mean, 'That's it?'" The speaker answered, "That's it. That is what you have to know." Then he continued.*

Once you know the definition of GDP and how it is measured, everything else falls into place. The economy becomes simple, because you are dealing with facts and definitions, not complicated theories.

# CHAPTER FOUR

# Rule #1: Facts Trump Theory

*The speaker put up a new sign:*
*Rule #1: Facts Trump Theory.*

Now that we all know what GDP is, and how it is measured, we can look at our bathtub economy.

We have a bathtub; and the water in the tub is Gross Domestic Product.

The water flowing in is:

> consumer spending,
> investment spending,
> government spending, and
> exports.

The water flowing out is:

> imports.

The actual quantity of water in the tub after some given time period depends on how much is coming in and how much is going out.

Whatever that is, it represents Gross Domestic Product.

In order to make it even simpler, imagine that the tub has marks on its side, like a measuring cup, so that we can easily know the quantity of water in the tub by looking at the water level.

And finally, to make the whole thing—our bathtub economy—as visual as possible, imagine there is a rubber ducky floating in the tub.

*As he said this, he threw a little rubber duck into the tub. The rubber duck bobbed along on top of the water.*

And so that you will never forget what we are doing here today, I am giving everyone his or her own rubber ducky to bring home.

*He took a canvas bag out of the little Austin Mini. The bag was filled with rubber ducks, and he threw them, one by one, into the crowd. When he saw that everyone had one, he continued.*

Just remember—the higher the rubber ducky is floating, the greater GDP is. As you can see, I have already opened the faucet and the drain on our tub. As I said, the water flowing into the tub represents consumer spending, investment spending, government spending, and exports. The water flowing out represents imports.

If I had opened the faucet more, while leaving the drain alone, there would be more water in the tub. If I had closed the drain more, while leaving the faucet alone, there would also be more water in the tub. In other words, the quantity of water in the tub, or GDP, is determined by the inflow and the outflow.

Of course, if we want the water gauge to measure the real quantity of water in the tub, we have to adjust for inflation or deflation, because rising prices can artificially raise the water level without increasing the actual quantity of water in the tub and falling prices can artificially lower the water level without decreasing the actual quantity of water in the tub.

And, once again, that's it.

Except for one more thing—money.

Our bathtub is a market economy with money, not a barter economy. In a barter economy, people trade things for things. In a market economy, people use money to buy goods and services, and they receive money for goods and services they sell, including their labor.

Market economies with money are more efficient than barter economies, because people simply use the money they have to buy what they want.

In terms of our bathtub, for the inflow and outflow to work efficiently, the entire plumbing system must be in tip-top shape. Therefore, we will have a master plumber represent the monetary authorities—the institution that controls the money supply.

If our plumber has the system running perfectly, we will not even think about the mechanics of the inflow and the outflow.

It is the same for the money supply. If the money supply is handled correctly, we will not even think about it.

But if the plumber lets us down, the flow of water in the system will not be efficient.

And if the monetary authorities let us down, by putting too little or too much money into the economy, the economy will be less efficient and GDP will suffer.

If they put too much money into the economy, we can end up with inflation.

If they put too little money into the economy, interest rates will increase and prices may fall, and the economy will not work as efficiently as it can.

Therefore, just as it is the responsibility of the master plumber to keep our plumbing system in order, it is the responsibility of the monetary authorities to keep the money supply in order—to ensure that we have just the right amount of money in the economy.

With our bathtub, the job of the master plumber is to make sure the system is working smoothly—to make sure all the pipes and faucets and drains are in order.

In the real United States economy, it is The Federal Reserve that has the responsibility of managing the money supply in order to ensure that the economy is working smoothly, which, according to the Fed, means having stable prices, sufficient economic growth, and an acceptable level of unemployment.

Of course, if we are going to talk about money, or the money supply, we should be clear about what we mean. Again, as with Gross Domestic Product, when we talk about money, we are talking about a definition. The most commonly used measure is M1, which is defined as coins and currency in circulation plus funds in checking accounts. In the textbooks, money in checking accounts is referred to as demand deposits, because it is available on demand. A broader definition of the money supply, M2, adds funds in savings accounts.

In most cases, when someone is talking or writing about the money supply, they are referring to M1.

In terms of numbers, more than 90 percent of the M1 money supply is made up of funds in checking accounts; less than ten percent is coins and currency in circulation.

# CHAPTER FIVE

# Rule #2: Reason Trumps Dogma

*The speaker put up another sign:*
  *Rule #2: Reason Trumps Dogma.*

*Then he continued.*

The beauty of America is that we are free to vote for politicians that serve our own greedy purposes, and against politicians that we think might serve the greedy purposes of others—possibly at our expense.

We seem to particularly like politicians who give us money. The problem is: We seldom get something for nothing, which, if you remember, is the number one rule of economics.

Or, to be accurate: We *never* get something for nothing.

That is why, no matter how you vote, and no matter how much you like the politician doing a little song-and-dance on stage, with a straw hat and a cane, claiming that his or her policy will help you, when you walk into work or talk with your broker, when you get down to business, you should keep your eye on the rubber ducky.

That is why I gave everyone a rubber ducky. Not only because it is a symbol of how the economy is doing, but because it is a reminder that when it comes to business, investing, and life, it is almost always better to ignore the quacks.

*Someone asked the speaker if he weren't simplifying the economy too much.*

*"The economy is simple," he said. "Of course, simple is not the same as simplification."*

If you think I am using a bathtub to simplify the economy so that everyone can understand something not worth understanding, I want to make it clear that I am not.

What is complicated is economics—the academic study of the economy. But our bathtub does virtually everything the elegant mathematical models do: It describes the real economy in a way that lets us understand how it works, and it allows us to explain and predict the results of changes.

Therefore, no matter how many *experts* are crowded around the tub talking about the value of complex theories, in the end, it all comes down to facts and numbers: Is the water level acceptable? Is the water level too low? Are there plumbing problems that need fixing?

In other words, no matter how many media gurus you see or hear, waving their hands and making great pronouncements, it is up to you to keep your eye on the rubber ducky.

*A woman standing next to the bathtub asked the speaker if he were going to use charts and graphs and numbers. She said she took two economics courses in college, and all she remembered were charts, graphs, and numbers.*

*He said, "None of that is necessary. As you will see, all you have to do is watch the rubber ducky."*

CHAPTER SIX

# The Right Amount of Water

*The next sign he held up read, "More is better."*

Okay. Water has been running into and out of our tub for about ten minutes. According to the water gauge, we have eleven and a half gallons in the tub.

*The speaker was standing on the trailer, next to the bathtub. He motioned for everyone to come up and take a look. "Well, what do you think?" he asked. "Looks right to me," someone said. The speaker laughed. "I don't mean, did I read the gauge correctly? What I am asking is: Do you think we have a good quantity of water in the tub?" Someone said, "Wouldn't more be better?" And the speaker said, "Very good. If the water is Gross Domestic Product, why wouldn't more be better?"*

We would obviously have more water in the tub if we increased the inflow relative to the outflow. But, no matter what we do, we are limited. There is a maximum quantity of water that can flow into the tub, and the most we can do to the drain is close it completely. So, if I had opened the faucets completely and closed the drain, there would be more water in the tub. Let's say that if I had done that, there would now be fifteen gallons of water in the tub.

*The speaker then asked what everyone thought about fifteen gallons versus eleven and a half gallons. "It has to be better," someone said. "Right," someone else said. "Very good," he said.*

Fifteen gallons must be better than eleven and a half gallons, because GDP is also a measure of national income.

But our bathtub shows us another obvious truth, which is that the level of GDP for a given time period is going to be limited by the available natural resources, technology, and work force.

Therefore:

Anything that increases the inflow relative to the outflow will increase GDP.

Anything that decreases the inflow relative to the outflow will decrease GDP.

As GDP increases or decreases, the rubber ducky will be bobbing higher or lower.

And we need just the right amount of money in the system, because the supply of money can affect both the inflow and the outflow.

But, no matter what we do, there is a limit to the level of Gross Domestic Product for any time period.

And we always have to be aware of the costs of what we do.

*The speaker then asked if there were any questions. There were. Following are the questions and his answers.*

# CHAPTER SEVEN

# GDP and Employment

*What about GDP and employment?*

The more water we have in the tub, the more employment we have.

GDP is the market value of all final goods and services produced inside the country during some time period, so it obviously requires more workers to produce fifteen gallons of water than to produce eleven and a half gallons. But is it enough? Will fifteen gallons of water give us full employment?

In the old days, meaning the days before the Great Depression, economists believed that a market economy would always reach an equilibrium with full employment, if we just waited long enough; even if that meant having to wait through long periods of low production and high unemployment.

The full-employment assumption and the *laissez faire* ideas it supported was described by the French economist J.M. Say (1767–1832) who argued that high levels of unemployment would eventually be cured by the forces of supply and demand. If there were seven gallons of water in the tub, and seven gallons of water resulted in a high level of unemployment, the solution, according to what became known as "Say's Law," was to wait—to wait for the water level to rise on its own as markets *cleared*—the assumption being that employment would increase because wages would fall.

The *political* corollary was that if government tried to fix such problems, it would only make them worse.[1]

The *laissez faire* idea was also based on the belief that production, not consumption, drives market economies. That belief led to the original supply-side economics idea, which was that if government wants to improve the economy, it should give breaks to business, not consumers, because if business profits increase, business will expand output, which will then increase employment and the incomes of workers.

Although the *guaranteed* full-employment assumption from the good old days is now seen as either false or useless, it was accepted by mainstream economists for many years—until the Great Depression made it clear that even if an economy might eventually recover on its own, it can be painful and costly to wait. Although many economists, even during the darkest days of the Great Depression, continued to argue that everything would eventually be okay, because in the long run, markets would clear, production would increase, wages would fall, and unemployment would disappear, others pointed out that, "In the long run, we are all dead."[2]

---

[1] Government can't solve the problem. Government is the problem.
[2] John Maynard Keynes

Given that is difficult to argue against the fact that, "In the long run, we are all dead," the Great Depression led to a revolution in economic thinking. Instead of continuing to believe that market economies are driven by production, virtually all economists decided that market economies are driven by spending, not production. More important was the belief that if there is an unacceptable level of employment, we should do something to fix it.

Most important, when the Great Depression ended, the government decided it should keep accurate statistics on the economy—collecting and publishing all sorts of data on prices, employment, and spending. As a result, in today's world, the decision to keep track of the real economy is more important than all the theories ever concocted, because it means that policies and decisions can be based on facts, not doctrine.

That is why it is important to understand that our bathtub is a description of economic definitions and facts.

It is also why theoretical arguments are now less important than economic facts.

And why Rule Number One is:

FACTS TRUMP THEORY.

# CHAPTER EIGHT

# GDP and Happiness

*How does GDP affect happiness?*

One of the goals of economics is to maximize the happiness, or wellbeing, of society. Unfortunately, no one has yet figured out how to measure happiness or wellbeing. So we measure real income instead, and assume that a higher GDP means greater happiness.

Obviously, that is not always the case, because, as we all know, there are many things other than money that affect our happiness; things such as health, safety, security, family, friends, art, education, meaningful employment, and the environment are just a few.

Therefore, in order to use GDP as an indictor of society's happiness or wellbeing we have to be clear what we mean. First, we assume that an increase in GDP will increase the wellbeing of society if, when GDP increases, no other factor or factors that affect happiness decline, or do not decline enough to offset the gain. Second, we assume that if GDP remains the same, or even increases, while other factors that affect happiness decline, then happiness may actually decline.

Two things come from thinking about happiness. One is a fact: It is that happiness cannot be measured solely in money terms. The other is a theory: It is that even if it is true that countless factors affect happiness, it is possible to create theories that can isolate individual factors and explain or predict how changes in just one, such as GDP, can affect the happiness or wellbeing of society.

# CHAPTER NINE

# Can We Fix A Bad Economy?

*Can we fix a recession?*

The elegant mathematical models presented in textbooks make it seem easy to fix a bad economy. So it is not surprising that the current view in industrialized nations is that when unhampered market forces do not create acceptable levels of profits, wages, and employment, we should do something to fix it. Of course, when I say "we," I am referring to either the government or The Federal Reserve System, which is the central bank of the United States.

Although those are the only two institutions with the power to "fine tune" the overall economy, the concept of using *pure* economic ideas to make the economy better is widely accepted by both economists and non-economists.

By the time World War II ended, virtually all rational people believed that if we could adjust the faucet and the drain to get more water in the tub, we should do it. Of course, as Shel Silverstein pointed out in his children's poem about a little blue engine that fails to chug to the top of a hill, even though it thinks it can, "*Sometimes, thinking you can just ain't enough.*"

In terms of our bathtub, the question is: Is it possible to increase GDP by intentionally changing the values of any of the variables—consumer spending, investment spending by business, government spending, exports, and imports?

Although the theoretical answer is an elegant, *yes*, the messy facts are not as certain.

# CHAPTER TEN

# Multipliers

*What is behind the elegant economic theories?*

One of the main reasons for creating complex theories that seem to offer more than the simple definition of Gross Domestic Product is a belief in multipliers. The idea of a multiplier is that if one of the components of GDP changes, there will be a change in GDP that is a multiple of the original. For example, if government spending increases by $1 billion, the multiplier effect says that GDP will increase by more than $1 billion. The number by which the change in government spending is multiplied in order to obtain the change in GDP is called the "spending multiplier." If the spending multiplier is 3, then a $1 billion increase in government spending will, in theory, lead to a $3 billion increase in GDP.

The question is: Why would an increase in government spending lead to a multiplied increase in GDP?

At the risk of giving everyone a headache, I am going to explain the idea of the multiplier, because multipliers are behind most of the theories that economists spend years studying, in course after course, and that are used for government policies and actions.

It may seem complicated, but it's not.

It is, once again, little more than using a definition. The definition is of what economists call the marginal propensity to consume. If you are old enough, you can probably imagine the comedian George Carlin staring into the camera and, with his eyes as wide-open as possible, saying, very slowly, "the marginal propensity to consume."

Aside from being a perfect line for a comedy routine, the marginal propensity to consume is the basis of the tax and spending multipliers that are the reason for believing that complex economic theories offer more than the straightforward definition of GDP.

The idea is that if someone receives an extra dollar of income, he or she will spend part of it and save the rest. The fraction, or percentage, of the extra dollar that is spent rather than saved, is called the marginal propensity to consume. For example, if people spend eighty percent of each additional dollar they receive, then if someone receives a $100 increase in after tax income, he or she will spend an extra $80.

Going back to the definition of GDP, if the government increases spending by $100, GDP increases by $100 (by definition). But the extra $100 spent by government also increases incomes by $100. Of course, the $100 increase in income does not add to GDP, because income is not one of the components of the definition of GDP. But, if the person who receives that $100 spends eighty percent of it ($80), then GDP increases by another $80, because consumer spending is one piece of GDP.

So, if government increases its spending by $100, GDP increases by $100 plus $80, which means the $100 increase in G leads to a $180 increase in GDP.

But, there is more. When someone spends an extra $80, that $80 becomes additional income to someone else, who, according to the theory, will spend 80% of it, or $64. And that $64 becomes additional income to someone else, who, according to the theory, will spend 80% of it, or $51.20. And so on. Each increase in consumer spending ($80, $64, $51.20, ...) is an addition to GDP, which means that the initial $100 increase in government spending leads to a multiplied increase in GDP.

Of course, each number in the sequence ($80, $64, $51.20, ...) is smaller than the previous number, because each number is 80% of the previous number in the chain.

Although this is, technically, an infinite chain, the sum of the increase in government spending plus each increase in consumer sending is, according to mathematics, equal to the change in government spending times the spending multiplier. And the spending multiplier is equal to one divided by one minus the marginal propensity to consume. Or, as George Carlin might say, "The spending multiplier is a number that is equal to the number one divided by the number one minus point eight, which is the number one divided by the number point two, which is the number five."

Although George Carlin's audience would, by now, be thinking that it might be a good idea to keep economists off the streets, economists, who have decided, on their own, to stay off the streets and away from the real world, want everyone to believe that the marginal propensity to consume idea gives us a multiplier number that can be used to predict the change in GDP due to a change in government spending.

If the marginal propensity to consume is 80%, the spending multiplier is 5.

If the marginal propensity to consume is 90%, the spending multiplier is 10.

Therefore, the more of their additional income people spend, rather than save, the greater is the spending multiplier.

The greater the spending multiplier, the more an increase in government spending will increase GDP and employment.

Like it or not, you have just been given the basics of the Keynesian model that is used to justify increases in government spending, tax cuts, and changes in interest rates intended to increase GDP and employment.

You may also have the headache I promised.

But, just to make sure you have a really good headache, you should know that the government spending multiplier is also used to predict changes in GDP due to changes in investment spending by business, as well as exports and imports. If the spending multiplier, calculated from the marginal propensity to consume, is 5, the theory says that an increase in investment spending of $50 million will increase GDP by $250 million.

Then there is the tax multiplier. The tax multiplier is used to predict how a change in taxes leads to a multiplied change in GDP. The tax multiplier is also calculated using the marginal propensity to consume, but it is numerically one less than the spending multiplier. So, if the spending multiplier is 5, the tax multiplier is 4. (Trust me.)

Now, back to your headache.

One way to cure a headache is to get rid of whatever caused it. In this case, if we get rid of the multiplier idea, we can ignore all the messy marginal propensity to consume calculations.

Of course, if we can legitimately get rid of the assumed importance of multipliers, we automatically diminish the importance of the elegant and complex economic models when it comes to real-world policies.

The question is: Can we legitimately get rid of the multiplier idea? The answer is: We can. All we have to do is look at the textbooks.

The textbooks used in principles courses present what is called a simple Keynesian model. In that model, the tax and spending multipliers are as described above. If the mpc (marginal propensity to consume) is .8, the spending multiplier is 5 and the tax multiplier is 4.

The textbooks used in intermediate and advanced undergraduate classes use intermediate models. In the intermediate models, the chain of additions to consumer spending set off by an increase in government spending is reduced by the assumption that the increase in economic activity will cause interest rates or prices to rise, either of which will cause a decrease in consumer spending. The result is a smaller multiplier. If the multiplier in the principles class were 5, the multiplier in the intermediate or advanced undergraduate class might be 3.

The textbooks used in graduate school offer advanced models. In the advanced models, it is understood that an increase in government spending, without an equal increase in taxes, increases the government deficit. And an increase in the deficit introduces factors, such as further increases in interest rates, that pretty much negate the increase in consumer spending predicted in the principles class.

So, by the time we get through the good graduate texts, the tax and spending multipliers are gone.

There is, however, one other multiplier everyone should understand. It is the "monetary" multiplier that is supposed to show how a deposit of new money in a bank leads to a multiple expansion of the money supply through the banking system. The monetary multiplier is based on the fact that banks are required to hold only a fraction of new deposits as reserves and are allowed to use the rest to make loans, which is what banks do to make profits.

The monetary multiplier (trust me, again) is equal to one divided by the legal reserve requirement. If banks are required to hold 10% of new deposits as reserves, the monetary multiplier is 10, which means if $100 of new money is deposited in a bank, there will be a $1,000 increase in the money supply.

The reason economists think the monetary multiplier is important is because changes in the money supply affect interest rates, and changes in interest rates affect consumer spending and investment spending by business, two of the components in the definition of GDP.[3]

But, as with the tax and spending multipliers, if we follow the textbooks, from principles classes to graduate school, the monetary multiplier gets smaller and smaller.

If the monetary multiplier in a principles textbook is calculated to be 10, it is smaller than 10 in the intermediate or advanced undergraduate textbooks, and it virtually disappears in the graduate textbooks. Why? Because the more accurate we are when looking at how the banking system works, the more leakages we see in the theoretical creation of money.

So, where are we?

We are back to the simple definition of GDP.

Which means no headache, because we do not have to worry about multipliers, or what economists call multiplier effects.

---

[3] To be accurate, a change in interest rates also affects imports and exports, two other components of GDP.

# CHAPTER ELEVEN

# Tax Cuts

*Do tax cuts increase GDP?*

I hate to talk about tax cuts, because there is nothing I can say that will not make someone mad. Maybe everyone. But the facts are simple:

Democrats like tax cuts they think will help their friends.

Republicans like tax cuts they think will help their friends.

Each claims its tax cuts will help the economy.

Republicans like the trickle-down argument.

Democrats like the trickle up argument.

If either Democrats or Republicans were correct, tax cuts would be a great idea. Your side wins first; then the economy improves; then the other side wins.

So, what's the problem? There is obviously a problem, because Democrats really hate Republican tax cuts and Republicans really hate Democratic tax cuts.

Is it just a problem of who wins first? Or most? Not exactly. The problem is reality.

A long time ago, Milton Friedman explained why the Kennedy tax cut did not help the economy. His reason was that a tax cut creates a government deficit before it can lead to increased spending by consumers (the Democrat idea) or increased spending by big business or rich guys (the Republican idea).

As such, unless you choose to live in a world of make believe, you know that deficits have to be covered. And there are only a few ways to do it: raise taxes, cut spending, or borrow (sell bonds). According to Friedman (and anyone who has graduated from the first grade), each choice works against the hoped for gains from the tax cut.

Cut taxes; raise taxes.

Cut taxes; cut spending.

Cut taxes; borrow and raise interest rates.

No matter which choice the government makes, the negative impact on the economy of financing the deficit negates the expected benefit of the tax cut.

As Friedman explained, there is one way out. That is to finance the tax cut by selling bonds that the Federal Reserve buys with newly created money. That way, interest rates do not increase, and the hoped-for boosts in spending and investment are not cut off.

As such, as Friedman explained, it is the increase in the money supply, not the tax cut, that helps the economy. The drawback is that the money creation risks inflation.

Years later, talking as a Republican rather than an economist, Friedman said he never met a tax cut he didn't like. Not because tax cuts help the economy, but because he believed tax cuts might lead to smaller government.

Therefore, those who like small government will ignore Friedman's academic work and focus only on his political statements. But if you stick with Friedman the academic, tax cuts are not likely to help the economy.

In today's new world, there is a new issue. It is that tax cuts are now routinely financed by selling bonds to foreigners. As a result, tax-cut deficits no longer cause automatic increases in interest rates. But, and this is the not-so-good part, deficit spending means owing a lot of our future wealth to foreigners.

*According to the textbooks, tax cuts always increase GDP.*

That's true for undergraduate textbooks. It is not true for good graduate texts. The reason is that the models in principles books ignore the deficit created by either a tax cut or an increase in government spending.

Most textbooks also ignore the fact that when an economy is in a recession, consumers are more careful with their spending, which means that the expected or predicted increase in spending caused by a tax cut may be countered by a decrease in spending as consumers adjust to poor economic conditions and negative expectations.

Finally, the models in principles texts do not take account of the fact that in a global economy, some of the increase in consumer spending is used to purchase things produced in other countries, which also diminishes the expected multiplier effect on GDP.

In the end, any increased inflow to our tub caused by a tax cut, is offset by a decrease in the inflow caused by whatever the government does to cover the deficit created by the tax cut. Or it has to be paid back out of future wealth.

While one hand is opening the faucet, the other hand is closing it, which is why a tax cut may not increase the water in the tub.

If, on the other hand,[4] the Federal Reserve buys bonds in the bond market, interest rates may not increase. But when the Fed writes checks to buy bonds, it increases the money supply, which may cause inflation. That is why a tax cut financed with money creation has a better chance of improving the economy. But, if that happens, it is because of the increase in the money supply, not because of the tax cut.

---

[4] President Harry Truman, after listening to hedged advice from a number of economic advisors, wished he could talk with a one-armed economist.

*A woman in the front row complained that the speaker was being political. "The reason my husband and I are here," she said, "is because we wanted to hear an economist, not a politician, talk about the economy. And you are taking the Democratic position on tax cuts, saying they don't work."*

*The speaker smiled. "Tax cuts are always political, because they are handed out by politicians. And politicians tend to pass tax cuts they think will help their own friends, which is why Republicans don't like Democratic tax cuts and Democrats don't like Republican tax cuts. When Democrats pass tax cuts, claiming they are helping the economy, Republicans say they won't work. When Republicans pass tax cuts, claiming they will help the economy, Democrats say they won't work. The argument I just gave you is the non-political economic argument. But it is not my argument, and it is not a Liberal argument; it is an argument first made by Milton Friedman, a conservative economist, in response to the Kennedy tax cut in the 1960s."*

# Government Spending

*Can increasing government spending improve the economy?*

In theory, a change in government spending is pretty much the same as a change in taxes. The one difference is that an increase in government spending adds directly to GDP, because government spending is one component of GDP.

Because of that difference, the simple models have a government spending multiplier that is larger than the tax multiplier.

But, as we already know, the simple models are not too good, which means the addition to GDP from an increase in government spending is also questionable.

However, aside from not recognizing the negative impact of the deficit, the theory of government spending makes an even more serious error. That error is to underestimate the real benefits of government spending by treating government spending as an abstract concept, rather than by describing exactly what the spending is to be used for.

That error leads economists and politicians to talk about changes in government spending without listing the exact benefits that are likely to result from exactly what the money is being spent on or taken away from.

For example, it is commonly assumed that it was a large increase in government spending that brought an end to the Great Depression. The problem with that assumption, aside from the fact that, because it is vague, it leads to loud arguments between liberals and conservatives, is that it ignores the fact that when the government spent money, it was spent on specific, identifiable things.

Looking back at the Great Depression, the huge increase in government spending on the war put people back to work. However, when the war ended, many experts feared that the U.S. would slip back into the depression that had been temporarily halted by WW II.

But, by design or luck, when the war ended, the U.S. government undertook some of the smartest spending in the history of the world.

One of the best was the GI Bill, which may have been implemented simply to reward those whose sacrifices helped save the free world.

But here is what the GI Bill actually did. It gave GIs an opportunity to earn a free college education and to purchase a house with a small down payment and low, below-market mortgage rates.

Those two things ended the Depression and catapulted America into its leadership role in the world.

And the government made a profit on the program.

As such, anyone who wants to look for ways to pull an economy out of a recession should look carefully at the GI Bill.

It made America the most educated country in the world.

It laid the foundation for America's supremacy in the sciences, as well as in the arts.

It created the largest middle-class of any industrialized country.

It created a country with the highest percentage of homeowners in the world.

It built America's suburbs, which some might see as a mixed blessing.

It led to the building of roads to service the suburbs.

It led to the creation of businesses to service a population that was spreading out from the old city centers.

It led to the growth of the American automobile industry, and to countless related industries.

And to American industry as a whole.

Very simply, the GI Bill can be credited with making the United States the number one country in the world.

Years later, statisticians compared the income taxes paid by those who received free college educations with the income taxes they would have paid had they not gone to college. The difference in taxes collected versus what would have been collected was a huge multiple of the cost of the program, which means the government earned a massive return on its investment. And make no mistake—the GI Bill was an investment; it was not undefined government spending. In fact, large parts of what is called government spending are investments in America that return more than they cost.

Then, in the 1950s, President Eisenhower began the construction of America's freeway system—the interstate connection that may have been initiated for national defense purposes, but which was responsible for huge increases in America's Gross Domestic Product.

This is important stuff, because it is necessary to understand that every dollar of government spending goes to an identifiable someone—whether it is an individual or a company—for some identifiable purpose. Anyone who ignores that fact and chooses, instead, to believe political dogma might be led to think that all government spending is nothing more than throwing taxpayers' money down a hole; which is not the case; which is why government spending is far more important that it appears to be in the elegant theories.

*So, increasing government spending can end a recession?*

It can. And it has.

Not because of an increase in "undefined" government spending, meaning spending on *anything*, but because of an increase in spending where the positive results of the investment can be clearly identified and listed.

For example, think of what could have happened if the government, at the beginning of 2009, in the middle of a significant recession, had decided to design an automobile that achieved 100 miles per gallon. Or an electric car with a two hundred mile range. The investment, which would have been similar to deciding to go to the moon and back, would have yielded enormous benefits. If, after the government completed the design work, private industry then put the designs into production, there would be a number of easily predictable benefits.

America's dependence on imported oil would virtually disappear.

The political situation in the Mideast would be changed forever.

People would have more money to spend on other things, because they would spend less on oil and gas.

A major cause of global warming would be reduced.

The economy would expand.

And America would have a new industrial base.

CHAPTER THIRTEEN

# Monetary Policy

*Can monetary policy improve the economy?*

Monetary policy means changing the money supply and interest rates in order to change consumer spending and investment spending. In theory, it has a better chance of success than tax cuts or increased government spending, because changing the money supply (or the rate of growth of the money supply) can change the inflow into the tub without creating a deficit that will offset the positive impact of lower interest rates. And the Federal Reserve can act immediately, without waiting for a Congressional debate.

Although economic textbooks go to great lengths to present the arcane process economists cooked up to explain how the money supply is increased or decreased through a fractional reserve commercial banking system, the truth is much simpler. If the Federal Reserve wants to increase the money supply, it purchases bonds in the open market with checks it writes from its own account, which means it creates new money out of thin air. If the Federal Reserve wants to decrease the money supply, it sells bonds in the open market, which means taking money from those who purchase the bonds.

Checks are money; bonds are not. Therefore, when the Fed buys bonds, it puts something that is money—Federal Reserve checks—into the economy and takes out something that is not money—bonds. When it sells bonds, it puts bonds into the economy and takes money out.

The theoretical results in the simple models are clear. If the Federal Reserve increases the money supply and lowers interest rates, consumer spending and investment spending increase. If the Fed decreases the money supply, interest rates increase, and consumer spending and investment spending fall, thereby decreasing the inflow into our tub.

That's it. It is just that simple—in the simple models.

The fact is, however, that lowering interest rates in the middle of a recession may not lead to the predicted increases in consumer spending or business investment. The reasons are obvious: People and businesses are more careful about borrowing when the economic outlook is bleak. Even at a zero rate of interest, a loan has to be paid back. And people without jobs, or who fear losing their jobs, are not as likely to borrow for purchases that can be put off. Even at a zero rate of interest, someone who buys a $30,000 car owes $30,000.

Does that mean no one will take advantage of low interest rates? Of course not. It means only that during a recession, increases in spending and investment are likely to be less than predicted by the simple models. And not guaranteed.

# CHAPTER FOURTEEN

# Monopoly

*Can regulating monopolies improve the economy?*

Yes. Market failure, such as the monopolization of markets, distorts prices and reduces economic efficiency, which lowers real incomes and consumer spending, which reduces the quantity of water in the tub.

Imagine what would happen if a single company took over the water supply in our bathtub. By controlling the entire supply of water, that company, as a monopolist, could limit the supply of water in order to get us to pay higher prices so that it can increase its profits. We lose, because we have to pay more for water than we would pay if there were competition in the market. We also buy less water, and we may buy more or less of other things than we would if prices were not distorted by the monopolist.

That is why correcting market failure with anti-trust legislation or price controls can increase economic efficiency, incomes, consumer spending, and GDP.

# CHAPTER FIFTEEN

# Positive Externalities

*Can correcting positive externalities improve the economy?*

Yes. Positive externalities are the benefits we receive when others spend their time or money to do something. Positive externalities exist when there are no markets for the benefits, because, if there is no market, we do not have to pay for the benefits.

Imagine that someone pays a fee to take a bath in our tub. He is now cleaner and smells much better. He feels good; so does everyone who comes in contact with him. But what if this person can afford to pay for only one bath a year? Would everyone who comes in contact with him on a daily basis feel better if he could pay for more frequent baths? Probably. Would each of them be willing to chip in a little money so he can take a bath every day? Probably. How much? That is a difficult question to answer. But if we know that each person would be willing to pay something, then we know that if we collected "taxes" from each of those people and used the money to pay for his daily baths, everyone would be better off.

In economic terms, whenever prices do not represent the true benefits of consumption or production, the private market solution results in too few resources being used for actions, such as education or inoculation against infectious diseases, that give positive benefits to others.

That is why correcting positive externalities with government production or subsidies increases economic efficiency, real incomes, consumer spending, and GDP.

# CHAPTER SIXTEEN

# Negative Externalities

*Does protecting the environment hurt the economy?*

Protecting the environment can improve the economy. Imagine that you want to take a bath in our tub. Just before you get in, you see that someone has dumped a bunch of dirt and garbage into it. You are upset, but you can't do anything about it. If you do not own the tub or the water in the tub, anyone can legally dump whatever he or she wants to into the tub. Does that affect your happiness or real income? Of course.

Why would someone dump garbage in the tub?

Possibly because it is the cheapest way for them to get rid of their garbage if there are no laws against such actions.

And, as we all know, not everyone cares about the negative impact their actions have on others.

What can you do? You can either take baths in garbage-filled water or you can decide to not take any more baths. In either case, you are worse off than if you could have stopped the dumping. If you owned the water, you could have made the dumper pay for the right to dump his garbage. How much? That depends on you. If you want to take baths in clean water, more than anything else, then there is no amount of money that the dumper could pay you for the right to dirty up your water. On the other hand, would you be willing to give up clean baths in return for $100,000,000?

In a true free market, there would be some sort of negotiation between you and the dumper that would arrive at a price you are willing to accept to give up clean baths in that tub and what he is willing to pay to dump his garbage in that tub rather than bring it somewhere else.

When the negations are done, you will have either clean water or dirty water and a bunch of money. It is up to you (and the dumper). Of course, it is unlikely that the dumper would be willing to pay $100,000,000. But in the real world, the numbers regarding damages, waste treatment, and costs of cleanup get pretty large.

That is why correcting negative externalities with laws that outlaw activities or with fines and taxes that make polluters responsible for the damages they cause to others increases economic efficiency, incomes, consumer spending, and GDP.

Some believe that taxes or fines on negative externalities, such as pollution, hurt the economy. That is not true. Taxes or fines, if they are based on the real damages caused by harmful actions, improve the economy, because one of two things happens. If the cost of reducing the damage is less than the true value of the damages, the polluter will fix the problem and avoid the fine. If the cost of reducing the damage is more than the true value of the damages, the polluter will pay the fine instead of correcting the problem. In either case, if the fine represents the true value of the damages, the economy wins. It is the true free market at work.

Environmental damage, such as pollution that harms people, occurs because markets do not exist for things such as air quality, water quality, noise, and so on. If markets do not exist, people or companies that cause pollution are not financially responsible for the damages they cause to others. And if consumers or producers are not responsible for the total costs of their actions, they will do more of those things than they would if they had to pay or compensate the damaged parties.

Meanwhile, if there are no laws to prevent such actions, the damaged parties cannot legally force the polluters to stop or reduce their pollution. The result is distorted prices that benefit polluters and negatively impact those who are hurt by the pollution—which is why economists call such actions *negative* externalities.

And because negative externalities reduce economic efficiency, correcting those externalities can increase incomes, consumer spending, and the water in the tub.[5]

---

[5]When people and companies spend money in markets with price distortions caused by negative externalities, the nation's resources are misused. The reason is simple: If prices do not represent the true costs of consumption or production, too many resources will be used for actions that cause pollution, and too few for actions that do not cause pollution.

CHAPTER SEVENTEEN

# Common Property Resources

*Does managing resources that are not owned help or hurt the economy?*

It helps.

Imagine that there are fish living in our tub. If we want to catch some fish every year, we could talk with someone who understands the biology of fish populations and find out how many fish we can catch this year, in order to have a healthy population that will let us catch fish year after year. The problem is: If we do not own the fish in the tub, someone else can come along and grab them all. In that case, the fish population is used up all at once, and there is nothing left for the future.

Who wins? The grabber? Maybe. Maybe not. Maybe the grabber also prefers to catch some fish every year rather than take them all at once. Why doesn't the grabber do what he wants to do, which is to catch a few fish each year? Because he knows that even if he tries to be careful, some other grabber can come along and take all the fish. Or maybe take so many that we have to catch fewer fish in the future if we do not want to fish the population to extinction. Therefore, we lose. We lose, because someone took all the fish, which means we no longer have the opportunity to catch fish as part of our overall consumption or spending plans.

How do we know we are worse off? There is a little test. Begin by recognizing the different possibilities. In this case, there were fish in the tub, and then there were no fish in the tub. Then look at the choices. When there were fish in the tub, we had two choices—catch some fish or catch no fish. When there are no fish in the tub, we have no choice—we cannot catch any fish. The question is: If, when there were fish in the tub, did we have the option of doing what the second possibility allowed, which is to not catch any fish? If the answer is, yes, then we did have that choice, but if we chose to spend the time and money to catch some fish, then we must be worse off, because without any fish in the tub, we do not have the option of doing what we chose to do when there was a choice to either catch fish or not catch fish. This test can be used for virtually all changes.

Meanwhile, the economic problem is that a lack of ownership for common property resources distorts prices and reduces economic efficiency, which reduces real incomes, consumer spending, and the water in the tub.[6]

---

[6] Unowned resources, which economists call "common property resources," are resources that are not owned by anyone until they are grabbed or taken by someone. Examples are fish in lakes, rivers, and oceans. No one owns the fish, so anyone can catch as many as he or she wants. That is why correcting common property resource problems with quotas, fines, or taxes can increase economic efficiency, incomes, and GDP.

# CHAPTER EIGHTEEN

# Public Goods

*Does providing public goods help or hurt the economy?*

It helps.

Imagine that our bathtub is filled with a lot of good stuff that is ours for the taking, but the tub is ten miles away from us. How do we get there to get the good stuff? We can hop in the car we bought with our own money. But what about the road? What if we can drive only on roads we pay for ourselves? Few people have the money to pay for their own ten-mile road. The rest of us are stuck, unless government collects a little money from each of us and uses it to build roads we can all use. If that happens, we all win.

That is why, when government provides public goods, such as roads, national defense, national parks, police and fire departments, courts, copyright protection, patent protection, and protection of property rights, it increases economic efficiency, incomes, and GDP.

Public goods are things that cannot be provided at all by private markets or that cannot be provided in sufficient quantity to maximize the nation's wealth or wellbeing. Public goods are things that can be provided only by government, which is why the failure of government to provide public goods reduces economic efficiency, real incomes, and the water in the tub.

Wise government spending on public goods may be the best deal taxpayers ever get.

Almost no one disagrees with the idea that government must play a role in providing public goods. However, there is almost no agreement on just how much of each public good we "need" or on which things are truly public goods.

In a world with limited resources, whatever is spent on public goods is not available for private goods. Therefore, one of the most difficult questions to answer will always be: How much should be taken away from private consumption in order to increase the availability of public goods.

In other words: How should the nation's limited wealth be distributed between *private* and *public* goods? Private goods are things that are produced because people are willing and able to buy them themselves—houses, cars, toothpaste, clothes, etc. Public goods are things that we do not actually buy—or at least we do not pay the full price when we use them. National defense, education, and medical research are just three examples. The argument is that if government does not provide such goods, we would not get enough of them and we would, therefore, be worse off as individuals and as a nation.

Unfortunately, there is no "scientific" way to determine exactly what we *need* to spend on national defense or for medical research. So it is left to politicians and special interest groups to decide how each public good is treated, as well as to decide which things will be dealt with as public goods.[7]

Using our resources for national defense or medical research or education or job training adds to the total happiness or wellbeing of the nation. But reducing the opportunity to buy things in private markets takes away from our happiness.

Therefore, given that we can't get something for nothing, we, as a nation, must constantly deal with the tradeoff between private and public goods, each of which can add to the wealth of the nation and the happiness of individuals.

---

[7] In some cases, benefit-cost analysis can be used to help make decisions.

# CHAPTER NINETEEN

# Investment Spending

*Can we improve the economy by intentionally increasing investment spending by business?*

Maybe. The Federal Reserve can change interest rates. And, according to the undergraduate textbooks, if interest rates increase, investment spending decreases and the water in the tub decreases. On the other hand, if interest rates decrease, investment spending increases and the water in the tub rises.

The theory is based on the fact that in the real world, there are many different investment opportunities available, each with a different expected rate of return. If all possible investment opportunities were listed in order of their expected return, from highest to lowest, a line could be drawn at the current rate of interest. Investments with expected rates of return higher than the rate of interest could be undertaken by borrowing the necessary funds, because each would yield a profit. Investments with expected rates of return less than the current rate would be passed up, because it would not be profitable to borrow the necessary funds at that current rate of interest.

Therefore, the theoretical conclusion is that if interest rates fall, the cut-off line moves lower, putting more investments into the profitable-to-do category. On the other hand, if interest rates increase, the cut-off line moves higher.

The facts, however, are a little different. The theoretical relationship between interest rates and investment ignores the fact that investment by business depends not only on interest rates, but also on current and expected economic conditions. That is why reducing interest rates in the middle of a deep recession (in Japan and the U.S.) did not lead to increased investment by business.

# CHAPTER TWENTY

# Government Production and Regulation

*Do government production and regulation distort prices?*

Of course. Government interference always alters prices.

The question is: Is that good or bad? Some believe it is always bad if government actions distort prices. The fact is that when regulations correct market failures or reduce the risk that can exist in unregulated markets, government price distortions improve economic efficiency and increase the water in the tub by correcting the price distortions caused by market failures.

Government spending intended to increase employment is not as effective as some might hope. But government production of public goods, as well as government regulations that correct price distortions caused by market failure or externalities will increase the water in the tub.

To begin with, there is one great truth: Without government, there can be no private business, large or small. Without the protection of property rights, copyright protection, patent protection, enforcement of contracts, and all the other things government provides, from education to roads, there would be chaos. Instead of orderly and profitable business, there would be gun slinging, bullying, and terrorism.

A second great truth about the role of government was stated clearly by Milton Friedman, one of America's most conservative economists, when he presented an economic interpretation of Abraham Lincoln's quote that government is "to do for the people what needs to be done, but which they cannot, by individual effort, do at all, or do so well, for themselves."

Friedman's more academic explanation of Lincoln's description of the role of government in a market economy is:

"In such a free private enterprise exchange economy, government's primary role is to preserve the rules of the game by enforcing contracts, preventing coercion, and keeping markets free. Beyond this, there are only three major grounds on which government intervention is to be justified. One is natural monopoly or similar market imperfection which makes effective competition (and therefore thoroughly voluntary exchange) impossible. A second is the existence of substantial neighborhood effects, i.e., the action of one individual imposes significant costs on other individuals for which it is not feasible to make him compensate them or yields significant gains to them for which it is not feasible to make them compensate him, circumstances that again make voluntary exchange impossible. The third derives from an ambiguity in the ultimate objective rather than from the difficulty of achieving it by voluntary exchange, namely, paternalistic concern for children and other irresponsible individuals."

Friedman's conclusion is clear: True free markets can exist only with government protection and regulation. It is a conclusion that is shared by all real economists when they write or speak as academic economists.

In the real world, however, the actual level of government production and regulation is determined by politicians and is related to, among other things, the health of the economy. Some of these factors are under our control; some are not. Some are actually automatic. For example, during periods of high unemployment, government payments to individuals rise. And during wartime, government expenditures increase dramatically, which is why wars add to GDP, sometimes making a not-so-good economy look better than it is, especially if the war is financed with bond sales financed with new money creation instead of taxes.

Government spending on public goods, social programs, and subsidies, such as agricultural programs, changes as political parties change power.

In the end, the actual levels of government production and regulation are always a mixture of economic ideas, compassion (or lack of compassion), political doctrine, and favors to friends and special interests.

# CHAPTER TWENTY-ONE

# Exports

*Can we intentionally change exports?*

Yes and no.

Many things affect exports, such as producing goods and services that people and businesses in other countries want to purchase, international trade agreements that make it easier or more difficult for U.S. producers to sell to foreign buyers, foreign exchange rates, and interest rates.

Interest rates are important, because of international capital flows. When interest rates increase, U.S. interest-bearing securities become more attractive to foreign investors, which leads to additional purchases of U.S. securities by foreigners. But, in order to buy anything from the U.S., including investments (such as U.S. bonds), foreigners first have to convert their currency into U.S. dollars.

Therefore, an increased demand for U.S. investments increases the value of the dollar relative to other currencies, thereby making U.S. products more expensive to foreigners, which then reduces exports.

As such, rising interest rates can lead to a decrease in exports, because the increased value of the dollar relative to other currencies makes U.S. goods more expensive to foreigners, and an increase in imports, because the increased value of the dollar relative to other currencies makes foreign goods are less expensive to Americans.

Because exports and imports are affected by the same factors—trade agreements, the value of the dollar relative to other currencies, interest rates, and anything that makes the goods and services of one country look good or bad to consumers and businesses in other countries—it is common to bundle them together and talk about the trade surplus or deficit.

In our bathtub economy, we separate exports and imports in order to focus on the importance of each in terms of its impact on GDP. Most models use net exports, which are exports minus imports. If we did that, there would be an outflow only if there were a trade deficit. As such, looking at net exports covers up a lot of what is happening. Japan knew, and China knows, the importance of both exports and imports. Each built a successful economy by encouraging exports and minimizing imports. Neither followed the idea that unhampered "free trade" would maximize the nation's wealth.

There is, however, a negative side to an increase in exports. It is that a large increase exports can raise prices at home. As a result, some of the gains from increased exports may be offset by higher prices for many goods and services.

# CHAPTER TWENTY-TWO

# Imports

*Will a trade deficit automatically eliminate itself?*

In theory, yes. In practice, not necessarily.

When people talk about free trade, what they normally mean is the duty--free importation of goods and services produced in foreign countries, either by foreign companies or by U.S. companies operating in foreign countries.

Limiting imports reduces the outflow from our tub, which, if it is accomplished without reducing exports, increases GDP. But, it may do so at great cost. If you have $1,000 to spend, does it matter how you spend it? Of course it does. There are many ways to spend $1,000, each of which gives you a different level of "happiness." If you can spend it only on goods and services produced in your own country, you are not likely to be as happy as if you had choices from all over the world. That is the argument often used to support what are called free trade policies—because few people would say that they do not like the idea of having as many choices as possible or the chance to buy an imported television set or kitchen appliances for less than they have to pay for the same items produced domestically. The counter argument is that it does not matter how cheap TVs are to someone who loses his or her job to imports.

Foreign commerce is complicated, which is why so many people choose to use simple free-trade "theories" created in the 1800s to support a pro free-trade position.

Unfortunately, the old free-trade theories are based on models using two products, two countries, and one input—labor. What they show is that if each country uses different quantities of labor to produce each of the two products, then, even if one country can produce each product with less labor than the other country, each country can gain by specializing in the product it is relatively better at producing and then trading some of that product to the other country for some of the other product. The theory's conclusion is that doing so gives each country a greater total quantity of the two products than if each produced both by itself.

What do these theories have to do with a world where countless goods, each requiring a large number of inputs, are bought and sold, not traded, among a large number of countries? Nothing. They have absolutely nothing to do with real international commerce, where things are bought and sold in a world with huge differences in wages, capital costs, government regulations and subsidies. In the real world, the fact that your country buys things from other countries does not mean that other countries will buy anything from your country. And because exports do not automatically match imports, fast-growth countries, such as Japan in the twentieth century and China in the twenty-first, intentionally promote exports and limit imports.

Of course, limiting imports hurts the living standard of many people. The reason for the harm, or loss, is simple—much simpler than the knowingly false free trade theories. It is that the benefits of specialization are real.

Whether it is the occupational specialization described by Plato in *The Republic* in 360 BCE or the industrial specialization described by Adam Smith in *An Inquiry Into The Nature And Causes Of The Wealth* in 1776, it is clear that self-sufficiency, even if it is a chosen lifestyle, limits the real income or wealth of individuals and nations. That is a non-refutable fact.

But the fact that specialization gives individuals and nations more income and more stuff than self-sufficiency, does not change another fact, which is that the inflow to our tub increases as exports increase and decreases as imports increase. Therefore, managing foreign trade is a complicated issue.

Although it is true that specialization makes sense for individuals and for countries, it is also true that exports add to the water in the tub and imports reduce the water in the tub.

That is why foreign trade policies must be addressed by looking at the facts, because there are no elegant free trade theories.

# CHAPTER TWENTY-THREE

# Outsourcing

*Does outsourcing jobs improve the economy?*

We don't know.

Outsourcing jobs reduces costs and increases profits for some.

On the other hand, outsourcing jobs reduces investment spending, some incomes, and consumption, thereby reducing the water in our tub.

The question is: Will the decrease in production costs and lower consumer prices add more to GDP than the lost incomes and profits take away? In other words, do the gains outweigh the losses?

Part of the answer, of course, depends on where the savings on less expensive imported services (outsourcing) are spent. Will they be spent on domestically produced goods and services? Or on more imported goods?

As with all other import savings, it is never clear that the savings will be spent in a way that adds to real GDP. Anyone who assumes that the savings will lead to an increase in GDP sees outsourcing as a good thing. Anyone who assumes that the benefits of the savings will be more than negated by lost incomes and profits sees outsourcing as a bad thing.

Who is right? No one knows. What we do know is that there is no reason to accept either side's assumption without evidence to back it up.

# CHAPTER TWENTY-FOUR

# Inflation

*Someone asked the speaker for a definition of inflation.*

The standard definition of inflation is: constantly rising prices over time.

The most commonly used measure of prices is the Consumer Price Index. Second is the Producer Price Index.

However, there are two completely different reasons for the Consumer Price Index or the Producer Price Index to increase.

The CPI can be pulled higher by increasing demand. Or it can be pushed higher by increasing costs of production, such as rising oil prices.

If the CPI is pulled higher by excessive spending, it is a signal of a possible inflation.

But if the CPI is pushed higher by rising costs of production, it is a signal of a possible recession.

As simple as that fact is, the media, investors, businesspeople, even the Federal Reserve, do not seem to comprehend the difference. The most likely reason for the confusion is the old textbook idea that there are two types of inflation—demand-pull and cost-push. Demand-pull inflation was assumed to be the result of a rising demand for goods and services that pulls prices higher. Cost-push inflation was assumed to be the result of rising costs of production pushing prices higher.

Demand-pull inflation is real. Cost-push inflation is not.

When rising oil prices cause increases in the Consumer Price Index, it means we should be prepared to deal with a possible recession, not inflation. On the other hand, increases in the Consumer Price Index caused by a rising demand that pulls prices higher is a true inflation.

That is why the only thing that can fund an ongoing increase in aggregate demand is an excessive increase in the money supply, which, today, is almost always the result of the monetary authorities creating money to finance deficit spending by government.

More relevant is the historical evidence that shows that all the great inflations were caused by too much money.

Of course, there have been only about fifteen truly bad periods of inflation throughout history, beginning with an ancient Roman inflation created when the government made more and more coins out of the same quantity of precious metals so that it could buy more and more stuff. The greatest hyperinflation in history occurred in Germany after World War I when, from the beginning of 1922 to November 1923, the price level increased by a factor of 20 billion. How could prices rise so much? Not because incomes rose 20 billion times; but because the German government, which had been forced to pay reparations it could not afford to the allied forces after the war, printed massive quantities of currency to pay the debt.

Very simply, there is no historical example of a high rate of inflation caused by anything other than a huge increase in the money supply.

But it is not only increases in paper currency that cause inflation.

Even when precious metals are used as money or to back the printing of paper currency, inflation can be caused by manipulating the existing quantity of precious metals, which is what the Romans did, or by a large increase in precious metals holdings, which is what happened to Spain when it brought back gold and silver from the New World.

In the United States, there were high rates of inflation during the Civil War, when the government of the North and the government of the South each printed paper currency to pay for its war effort, and during World Wars I and II when the government financed war spending with money creation. But one of the worst U.S. inflations was from 1965 to 1980, when the government paid for both the Vietnam War and the War on Poverty at home by selling bonds that were bought by the Federal Reserve with new money creation. That inflation ended when Paul Volcker, the Federal Reserve Chairman who had created all the money, announced that the Fed was changing its policy and would, from then on, keep the growth of the money supply within narrow limits.

It is important to recognize that the inflations that occurred during WWI, WWII, and the Vietnam War were not the result of printing paper currency, but by the creation of checking account money as the Fed purchased government bonds in the bond market to fund government spending.

It is also important to understand that when the money supply is increased, it is not divided up among all the people. In other words, if you hear that the money supply increased at a ten percent annual rate last month, there is no need to call your bank to see if your checking account has magically increased. It has not. The new money ends up in the accounts of those who sold bonds, because they exchanged bonds, which are not money, for checks, that are money.

*What's wrong with the cost-push inflation theory?*

If prices are determined by supply and demand, then it seems to make sense to argue that greed is a major cause of inflation. But, it is not that simple.

The cost-push argument is that if costs of production increase, sellers will pass on the higher costs to its customers by raising prices. It sounds like a sensible argument. In fact, it is still included in some textbooks. But it has a serious flaw. It assumes that if production costs increase, a business can protect its profits by raising prices—an assumption that many corporations believe to be true.

But sellers cannot pass on all such costs. Anyone who sells something faces a demand for the product. If not, they would not be in business. If there is no demand, there is no business. But when a seller raises his or her price, consumers buy less of that product. As a result, any seller that increases prices in an attempt to recover higher costs of production will not sell as much, which means it will then cut back production, which means using fewer inputs, which means lowering other prices.

When it is all over:

The prices of products produced with higher costs of production will be higher, but output will be lower. Part, but not all, of the increased costs are passed on to consumers. Profits are lower, because less is being sold and production costs are higher. The lower production leads to unemployed resources. And as the unemployed resources look for new employment, wages and prices fall in other industries.

There are higher prices in the industry with higher production costs and lower prices elsewhere. But that is not inflation. It is a change in relative prices.

*Why can't sellers pass on higher costs by raising prices?*

If sellers could raise prices whenever they wanted, then why not raise them by more than enough to cover the higher costs? Even better, for the seller, why not raise prices every day and add to profits no matter what is happening to production costs? Why pass up the chance to make billions of dollars by keeping prices low?

In other words, why don't greedy businessmen constantly create inflation by charging higher and higher prices?

Because they can't. Not if they want to make a profit and stay in business.

One of the basic assumptions of economic theory is that everyone—individuals, unions, small businesses, and huge monopolies—will always try to get the most they can.

But there is a big difference between getting the highest price for something and making the largest profit. If a business could charge any price it wanted and sell all it wanted, anyone could start a business and make billions of dollars by charging one or two million dollars for each item they sell, whatever it is.

You could call yourself a consultant, charge one million dollars per hour for your services, and advise every financially troubled business to simply raise its prices. You could also advise every profitable business to raise its prices and make even greater profits.

These are obviously absurd ideas. So is the idea that a business has the power to charge whatever price it wants.

It is true that when resource costs increase (labor, oil, interest expenses, and so on) it is more expensive to produce products that use those resources, and the prices of those products will increase. But that is not inflation.

*What about the prices of things we need?*

Economists do not think you "need" anything. You might say that you need food to live. But you do not buy "food." You buy a certain kind of steak, a certain size and grade of eggs, a particular brand of orange juice or whole oranges, and so on. There is not one particular food item you, or anyone else, must have. So, whenever some prices increase, less of those goods and services are sold. At the same time, people look for substitutes, even if it is a different brand.

That is why it is impossible to present a logical explanation of how increasing resource costs create inflation. In each and every case, the upward pressure on prices is stopped by the fact no one has yet discovered an instance where it is possible to raise prices and sell the same quantity.

*Someone asked if inflation helps anyone.*

Inflation helps debtors, because they get to pay back their loans with money that is worth less than the money they borrowed. At the same time, inflation hurts lenders, because when the loans they made are paid back, they receive money that is worth less—in terms of what it can buy—than the money they loaned out. Therefore, there is a longstanding difference of opinion between debtors and creditors concerning inflation. That is what was behind William Jennings Bryan's "cross of gold" speech.

In 1896, after more than twenty years of declining prices, Bryan gave his famous speech at the Democratic National Convention in Chicago. The ending, which was a rebuttal to those who wanted the nation's money supply pegged to gold, was, "Having behind us the producing masses of this nation and the world, supported by the commercial interests, the laboring interests and the toilers everywhere, we will answer their demand for a gold standard by saying to them: You shall not press down upon the brow of labor this crown of thorns, you shall not crucify mankind on a cross of gold."

Bryan's populist argument was that the U.S. should have a bimetallic standard, using both silver and gold as backing for money. The reason for using both silver and gold is that it would allow more money to be created, thereby increasing the rate of inflation. Bryan was trying to help farmers and other working people who were large debtors, because they were being hurt by more than two decades of falling prices. If prices were increasing, instead of decreasing, the real burden of their debts would be reduced. Of course, bankers wanted to hold to the gold standard, because, as creditors, they benefited from stable or declining prices.

That is why Bryan ended his speech with an image of working people being crucified on a cross of gold. No matter which side you might support in the debate, the fact is that the relationship between money and prices has been understood for a long time.

An interesting idea that has been around for a while is that *The Wizard of Oz* is an allegory based on the populist movement in America; that it is a story that pits the workingman against big bankers and railroads. According to these interpretations, the story is filled with characters and locations and numbers that represent the people, places, and legislation involved in the populist movement. The cowardly lion is William Jennings Bryan. Oz, of course, is the symbol for ounce. In the book, Dorothy's slippers are silver, not ruby red. The yellow brick road represents the gold standard that leads to Oz (Washington DC). And the conclusion, where Dorothy finds out that she had the solution all the time, which is to click her heels together, represents the idea that the solution to the problem of declining prices is to add silver to gold as backing for money, which is a reference to the cross of gold speech. The movie loses this idea by changing the slippers from silver to ruby red.

One of the major articles that makes the above argument is "The 'Wizard of Oz' as a Monetary Allegory," by Hugh Rockoff in *The Journal of Political Economy*, volume 98, No. 4 (August 1999) pages 739 – 760.

*Someone asked how to explain inflation using the bathtub.*

It is easy to explain inflation using our bathtub.

We begin by assuming that the master plumber (The Federal Reserve) has just the right amount of money in the system (our tub); meaning that the system is working smoothly and prices are stable.

If the Federal Reserve then puts more money into the economy, we can imagine throwing bags of money into the tub. Each bag raises the water level, but not the real quantity of water. Therefore, the water gauge does not measure the real quantity of water. In order to keep track of the real quantity of water, the water level has to be adjusted to account for the inflationary price increases caused by having too much money in the tub.

If the Federal Reserve keeps throwing bags of money into the tub, eventually the tub will overflow, spilling GDP onto the floor. In other words, inflation not only raises prices, it eventually reduces real GDP.

So, once you understand the cause, the cure is simple.

Keep the money supply under control. Do not throw too many bags of money into the tub. And if inflation is a serious problem, take some bags out of the tub.

# CHAPTER TWENTY-FIVE

# Recession

*What about recession?*

A recession is an economic slowdown with unacceptable rates of unemployment, and often by falling wages, profits, and prices. The Great Depression was an extreme recession.

In general, there are two different kinds of recession: insufficient-demand recession caused by the bursting of speculative bubbles, large decreases in the money supply, or something that reduces production, employment, wages, and profits and cost-push recession caused by rising resource costs.

The Great Depression was triggered by the bursting of a speculative bubble in the stock market, and was turned into a depression by the Federal Reserve when it allowed banks to fail, the money supply to contract, and individuals to lose their savings.

The downturn that began in 2007 was triggered by rising oil prices in the summer of 2007 and turned into a deep recession when the speculative "investment" bubble tied to mortgages, derivatives, and credit-default swaps burst. As in the 1920s, it was a failure to regulate unwarranted speculation that created a bubble.

In terms of our model, it means not enough water in the tub.

In other words, a recession occurs when something reduces the quantity of water in the tub to a level that does not support full employment. It could be any number of things. An increase in oil prices, bad weather (the dust bowl days of the Great Depression), a disruption in investment, a decrease in the money supply, and so on.

Some of the causes are beyond our control, such as weather.

Some are human error, such as bad management of the money supply or a failure to regulate excessive speculation in financial markets.

Although it commonly believed that rising oil prices cause inflation, because higher oil prices cause increases in the Consumer Price Index and the Producer Price Index, that is not the case. The mistake is to focus on increases in the Consumer Price Index, which tracks the price of a bundle of goods over time, while ignoring the reason for the increase. High oil prices lead to higher production costs and higher prices for consumers. We know that. But because rising oil prices do not increase incomes, the quantity of goods and services purchased declines, which reduces production, employment, wages, and profits, which is a recession, not an inflation.

Therefore, whenever the Federal Reserve raises interest rates to stave off an inflation caused by rising energy prices, it is doing the opposite of what it should be doing, which is to act to prevent a recession.

# CHAPTER TWENTY-SIX

# The Business Cycle

*What about the business cycle?*

A lot of people spend a lot of time trying to explain and predict the business cycle.

There are obvious reasons for wanting to uncover the mystery behind the ups and downs in the economy. One is that anyone who can predict the future can make a lot of money. A more important one, for society, is that if the business cycle can be predicted, then actions can be taken to hopefully prevent bad things from happening to the economy and the people.

Although some business cycle theories look pretty good, such as those that attempt to tie the performance of the economy to a politically motivated presidential cycle, the real evidence supports the argument that there is no natural business cycle, just as there is no natural climate cycle. The evidence for such an argument is simple: Each and every upturn and downturn in the economy can be explained by actions or events that caused it. Therefore, if the causes for upturns and downturns can be explained, there is nothing left of a "natural" cycle.

# CHAPTER TWENTY-SEVEN

# The National Debt

*What about the national debt?*

From the end of World War II, many theories argued that the national debt was not a problem.

Before and during the Great Depression of the 1930s, it was assumed that the federal government had a responsibility to maintain a balanced budget. It was believed that government should act like an individual and that an individual in debt was an individual in trouble. The one exception was wartime, when it was acceptable for government to run a deficit as long as it was understood that the necessary borrowing would be repaid when the war was over.

But, as the Depression worsened, John Maynard Keynes, whose ideas still guide the teaching of economics at 90 percent of the colleges and universities in America, made the argument that if a nation were stuck in a depression, the government should use deficit spending as a cure. Although most people have heard of Keynes, and many conservatives blame him for the downfall of free-market ideals, few understand that what he offered was an entirely new way of seeing the economic world.

Following Keynes, and using 20/20 hindsight, economists at the end of World war II began to believe that trying to balance the federal budget had made the Depression worse, not better. The argument was simple. If people lost their jobs and their businesses, government lost tax revenues. If government then tried to balance its budget, it would have to reduce it's spending, which would cause more unemployment and further reductions in tax collections. The result is a vicious downward spiral. Fewer jobs mean less tax money. Less tax money means less government spending. And less government spending means fewer jobs. And on and on.

Prior to Keynes, economists assumed that as long as producers produced something, those who sold them the resources needed to make those things, whether it was labor or coal, would then have the money to buy what was produced. According to this view, "supply creates its own demand" and there is no role for the government to play in regulating the economy. Of course, if production were the key to economic health, the depression of the 1930s should not have occurred.

According to Keynes, the reason for the lengthy depression of the 1930s was that demand, not supply, is the driving force in the economy. As such, if total spending is not great enough to pull an economy out of a recession, it is the government's responsibility to generate a sufficient demand for goods and services, even if it has to use deficit spending. Then, as with a war, the government debt is to be repaid out of the tax revenues generated by a healthy economy.

It is sometimes believed that President Roosevelt was quick to adopt the Keynesian idea of massive deficit spending as a way to end the depression. But that was not the case. Although there was some anti-depression spending, Roosevelt and his advisors were limited by the continued belief in the importance of a balanced budget—until the U.S. entered World War II.

*What changed after World War II?*

After World War II, economics entered a new age.

There was, for the first time, a cohesive theory that explained, at least in broad terms, how government could regulate the economy through its impact on total spending.

There was the experience of World War II spending to back up the theory.

And there was a new attitude toward government debt. No longer did everyone believe that government must meet the same budget constraints as individuals. No longer did everyone see government debt as a threat.

Instead, economists believed they had the knowledge and the tools to create an economy that would grow steadily without suffering the tragic upheavals of either inflation or recession.

To those who continued to complain that debt was bad, no matter who owed the money, economists argued that government debt was not the same as private debt. The argument was that government debt, the outstanding bonds sold to finance past deficit spending, is "like owing money to yourself."

The debt was not supposed to matter because paying it off was "like taking money out of one pocket and putting it in another." When future taxes were used to redeem maturing bonds, the taxes would come from Americans and the payments would go to Americans.

Of course, the theoretical argument did have a loophole. Even if you "technically" owed the money to yourself, increasing the debt pushed interest rates higher. And high interest rates cause an economic slowdown.

*So the old idea that paying off the national debt is like taking money out of one pocket and putting it in another does not make sense?*

Not if large quantities of bonds are sold to foreigners, unless you want to think of it as having a hole in the pocket.

The Reagan deficits and the Bush deficits forced interest rates higher than they would otherwise have been, and those high rates brought in foreign investors.

The United States benefited by being able to use foreign money to help fund its large deficits without the negative consequences of higher interest rates.

The downside is that the money has to be repaid, with interest. Now when government taxes Americans to pay the interest on government bonds and to redeem maturing bonds, part of the money goes to foreigners. And now, when we pay off government bonds by taking money from one pocket and putting it in another, some of the other pockets are in foreign countries

*What new problems are related to foreign investment?*

There are at least three.

One: If foreigners hold a large part of our debt, they have a claim against our present and future wealth. Paying the interest on the debt, which is the third largest item in the federal budget, means sending money abroad. Redeeming bonds does the same. Therefore, when deficit spending is used to promote economic growth intended to benefit Americans in the future, some of the future benefits will be owned by foreigners.

Two: The huge federal debt is partly responsible for the growing foreign trade deficit. Massive government bond sales force interest rates higher and attract foreign investors. But in order to invest in the U.S., foreigners have to switch their currencies into dollars. The more money foreigners want to invest in the U.S., the more dollars they need. The more dollars they need, the more they push up the value of the dollar on foreign exchange markets. The stronger dollar makes foreign goods cheaper for Americans to buy and American goods more expensive to foreigners. The result is added pressure on the foreign trade deficit.

Three: The large U.S. debt, coupled with the growth of international investing, may reduce the effectiveness of domestic monetary policy. It is assumed that the Fed has the ability to increase the money supply, lower interest rates, and promote greater capital investment and consumer spending. But, as the foreign-held debt becomes larger and larger, we may reach a point where, if the Fed tries to raise total spending by forcing interest rates lower, foreigners might pull funds out of U.S. bond markets. As funds are pulled out, interest rates will increase. If that happens, the Fed may lose its ability to juggle interest rates to meet domestic economic needs. As a result, it may become difficult to use expansionary money-supply policies to encourage economic growth without risking inflation.

*Is this the end of an era?*

Beginning with the end of the 1950s, economists thought they had a handle on the economy. Even the soaring inflation of the 1970s can be traced to understandable policies: We fought two wars, a war on poverty and a war in Vietnam, and financed the efforts with money creation, not increased taxes.

But the policies we believed could be used to "fine tune" the economy—increasing or decreasing government spending, taxes, and the money supply—may now have to be reexamined. We are, very possibly, losing the control we once took for granted.

The United States is now the world's largest debtor nation—measured as the difference between the value of foreign debt owned by Americans and the value of American debt owned by foreigners. And although we understand the dangers of foreign debt in Brazil and Mexico, we do not always recognize that those countries are simply extreme examples of what could happen in the United States.

Whether or not it was ever accurate to say that the national debt does not matter, it certainly matters when a larger and larger portion of it is held by foreigners.

It matters because it means that foreigners have a legitimate claim to a part of our present and future wealth, which will reduce our standard of living in the future.

It also matters because GDP is based in part on our ability to manage our own economy; and our ability to do so may decline as our debt grows and more of it is owned by foreigners.

# CHAPTER TWENTY-EIGHT

# Economic Growth

*What about economic growth?*

We need economic growth to prosper as a nation, and as individuals.

Equally important is that the wealthier a nation is, the more opportunities there are to help those who need help or to provide solutions to problems that can make all of us or some of us better off.

If you asked twenty people to list what they believe are today's ten worst problems, it is almost certain that no two lists would be identical. But there is a good chance that some of the following issues would show up on every list: AIDS, illegal drugs, prescription drugs, the deterioration of the environment, poisons in our food, poverty, homelessness, unfair foreign trade, the spread of nuclear weapons, the fear of nuclear destruction. Some lists would also include either too much government regulation and too much government production or too little regulation and too little production.

No one would claim that all these problems are strictly economic problems. But each and every one is either directly or indirectly related to the performance of our economy and the economies of other nations.

Each problem could be lessened with greater economic growth, either because the greater wealth would give people more money or more hope, or because the greater wealth would give us more resources that can be devoted to solving our problems.

Of course, the creation of greater total wealth will not automatically funnel more resources into attempts to solve any of these problems or to increase the incomes of the poor. Also, spending more money on a particular problem does not guarantee a solution, and solving one problem while giving up something else will not necessarily increase the nation's total happiness or wellbeing

But, the wealthier we are as a nation, the better the chances are for dealing with our problems and the better the chances are for having all incomes increase.

*Can we intentionally generate economic growth?*

In our bathtub, the water represents GDP for a given time period, such as single year, which means that economic growth is represented by having more water in the tub year after year. Technically, economic growth should measure the change in GDP per person, not just in total. And that requires a greater inflow each year, just to keep up with a growing population.

*What causes economic growth?*

That is one of the most important questions in all of economics. The question, which is of crucial importance to both developed and developing nations, is also the least understood in all of economics.

Academic journals and textbooks are filled with all sorts of explanations and theories of economic growth, each of which is of little or no value in the real world.

Does that mean economists do not know anything about economic growth, in particular, how to encourage positive growth? The answer is, no. Economists have known for more than two thousand years what the key to economic growth is. But, to be useful, that knowledge must be separated into two somewhat distinct categories—economic growth in underdeveloped (or developing) countries and economic growth in developed countries (which we hope will continue to develop). The reason for the distinction is that there are important differences between developing and developed countries.

*What causes economic growth in developing nations?*

There is a clear list of factors that leads to economic growth in underdeveloped countries.

1) The first factor, which was explained brilliantly by Plato in *The Republic* (360 BCE), is specialization. So far, no one has done a better job than Plato of explaining the incredible benefits of specialization in a pre-industrialized economy. As people move from being self-sufficient individuals or families—meaning that they produce everything they need by themselves—to specialized producers, such as wheat growers, shoe makers, candle makers, or pin makers, a whole market economy develops. Specialization in production lets people produce far more of a single product than they can use themselves, thereby giving them the opportunity to sell some or all of what they make and buy what they need and want. The result is that people and families end up with much more than they could ever produce by themselves. Out of this specialization, markets develop where things are bought and sold—using money, not barter. Then come retailers, wholesalers, and foreign trade. It is all described in *The Republic*. And it is such specialization that is the single

most important reason for massive increases in economic growth and the wealth of the nation.

2) The second factor, which was described by Adam Smith in 1776, is specialization in factories. Smith took Plato's description of specialization in a pre-industrialized economy and brought it into an industrialized economy. In Smith's pin factory example, workers specialize in making one part of a pin. Instead of Plato's pin makers, who, by specializing in making pins, might make 20 pins a day, each of Smith's pin makers, working in a factory, makes the equivalent of 200 pins a day. (In Smith's example, ten workers in a pin factory turn out 2,000 pins a day, versus the 20 he assumed each can make on his own.) It is described wonderfully in Smith's *An Inquiry Into The nature And Causes Of The Wealth of Nations*. And it is the single most important reason for massive increases in economic growth and the wealth of nations that Smith predicted.

3) The third factor is the need for capital to fund the factories that allow the specialization described by Adam Smith. In many developing countries, that capital is difficult or impossible to find. In developed countries, investment in capital goods occurs when some current production is directed toward the creation of productive facilities and infrastructure. In poor nations, there may not be enough current production to meet basic needs—such as food and shelter—which means it is virtually impossible to free up production to build for the future. In such cases, the needed capital must come from somewhere else. However, it is difficult for benevolent nations to provide capital goods to improve future conditions when millions of people may be starving today.

4) The fourth factor is property rights, because in order for factors one through three to be implemented, it is necessary for people to have property rights to protect

what they have. Without property rights, neither Plato's nor Adam Smith's specialization can take place, because without property rights, everything can be taken away from anyone who prospers. And, in both developing and developed countries, if contracts are not enforced and protected, virtually everything is handed over to those with the brute force to take what they want from everyone who is weaker.

5) A fifth factor is stability—a stable government and a stable economy—because without stability, investment cannot take place in either Plato's or Adam Smith's world. Again, in many poor nations, there is no stability. There is, instead, chaos and civil war.

*What causes economic growth in developed nations?*

The first four factors listed above are already present in developed nations, which is why a reasonable rate of economic growth is the norm.

The fifth factor is also present, but it can vary. Although most developed nations have stable governments, there are times when that is not the case. And although most developed countries have relatively stable economies, that is also not always the case.

Even the most developed countries suffer bouts of inflation and recession, each of which is detrimental to economic growth.

And even the most developed countries experience periods of low saving rates, outside economic disruptions, and bad government policies that can disrupt the normal and expected rate of economic growth.

On the other hand, there are also periods of beneficial change, such as times of significant increases in technology that push economic growth above its expected level.

Therefore, the most important factors for encouraging economic growth in developed countries are economic stability, and wise policies by governments and central banks.

In terms of our bathtub, here is what we know:

Specialization increases the water in the tub.

Avoiding inflation and recession increases the water in the tub.

Correcting market failures and externalities increases the water in the tub.

Education increases the water in the tub.

Property rights increase the water in the tub, because property rights are a necessary part of economic growth, which is why so many underdeveloped countries suffer from limited or no growth.

Too little money in the economy raises interest rates, which decreases the water in the tub.

Too much money in the economy can cause inflation, which decreases the water in the tub.

A foreign trade surplus adds to the water in the tub.

A foreign trade deficit reduces the water in the tub.

Economic growth requires that some resources that could be used for current consumption be invested, instead, in human and physical capital, thereby increasing the capital base and the productivity of the economy. Because of this, it is difficult or impossible for countries that cannot afford to give up any current consumption, because it is needed for survival, to grow without outside help.

But, we would like to know more. If there is one question economists would like to have answered, it is: What more can we do to intentionally increase the rate of economic growth in both developed and developing countries?

# CHAPTER TWENTY-NINE

# The Japanese Economic Miracle

*How can you explain the Japanese economic miracle without tying it to a free trade policy?*

The Japanese economic miracle is not an example of the benefits of *free* trade; it is an example of the gains from *controlling* foreign trade. The huge economic expansion in Japan began with a massive decline in world shipping costs that took place during the later half of the twentieth century; but it owed its existence to a policy that promoted exports and restricted imports. While Japanese automobiles and other Japanese products poured into the United States, Japan blocked many imports. Therefore, while Japan's economic miracle occurred while it was protecting and promoting manufacturing at home and running a large foreign-trade surplus, its economic decline can be traced to the time when its trade surplus began to fall—when Japanese manufacturers began to move production out of Japan and into China, Korea, Indonesia, even the United States.

*And you blame that on free trade?*

It was no coincidence that the decline began when Japanese companies began moving manufacturing out of Japan. Or that it was then that many Japanese workers went from having jobs for life to being unemployed. Adding to the problem, of course, was a reduction in the exports of manufactured products caused by the growing weakness in world markets.

# CHAPTER THIRTY

# The Chinese Economic Miracle

*What about the fast rate of economic growth in China?*

China, in the twenty-first century, is doing exactly what Japan did in the twentieth century. It is encouraging exports and limiting imports, thereby expanding manufacturing by Chinese companies, many of which are manufacturing things for American companies that are than shipped to America. A few years ago, it seemed as though every product you picked up said, *Made in Japan*. Today, almost everything you see says, *Made in China*.

*What does that have to do with the United States?*

The United States is also one history's great economic miracles. For many years, it benefited from the *protectionist* existence of two oceans and high shipping costs. As such, it was an economic miracle with minimal foreign trade that was fueled by vast quantities of valuable natural resources. But it is at risk if its manufacturing base shrinks.

Restricting the supply of imports from other countries hurts consumers, because prices are higher and fewer products are available.

But we cannot sacrifice everything for the chance to spend all our money today on cheap imports. It's like the children's story of the ant and the grasshopper. As individuals or nations, if we spend everything today, we are risking a bleak tomorrow. According to economics, real economic growth takes place only if current consumption is *not* maximized. Some current consumption must be exchanged for the build-up of manufacturing capabilities. That's why we need foreign trade policies that help us prepare for the future, not policies that let us freely spend our way into poverty while increasing the profits of a few.

One way or another, we pay for what we buy today. While the Japanese economy was expanding, the Japanese had a high standard of living. Even though Japan, especially Tokyo, was one of the most expensive places in the world to live, high wages made up for the high prices.

*You sound like a protectionist.*

No, I'm an economist. And economists worry about what things really cost—not what they appear to cost. What is the real cost of imports? It is not just what we pay at the time. It is what we have to give up to buy them. That includes the price, but it also includes the loss of future wealth if it leads to the loss of manufacturing in America. In economic jargon, it is called opportunity cost. Opportunity cost is defined to be the value to you of what you must give up when you buy or do something. In the case of trade policies that encourage American companies to move manufacturing out of America, the lower prices of imported goods means that we are consuming our wealth. It's like never changing the oil in your car. You save money for a while. Then the car breaks down. We need to keep the car running. That will not happen if we fail to understand the true cost of free-import policies. And it cannot happen without wise government actions aimed at maximizing the wealth of the nation.

# CHAPTER THIRTY-ONE

# A Little More Free Trade Theory

*Isn't free trade the sacred cow of economics?*

It is. It is an idea that economists are not supposed to question. However, we already know that exports add to GDP and imports subtract from GDP. Therefore, the facts are that a foreign trade surplus increases GDP and a foreign trade deficit decreases GDP.

Given those facts, the question is: What is the purpose of the assumed-to-be-airtight economic theory of free trade that is based on the idea of comparative advantage?

The answer appears to be that its purpose is to support what are called free trade policies or free trade agreements with other countries. In particular, it is claimed that the theory of free trade is all the "proof" we need to argue against any and all restrictions to the free importation of goods and services.

The problem is that the theory is not so good. It is an airtight argument only for one special case—the case where there are two countries, two things to produce, and each country has different relative costs of production. Given those conditions, the theory concludes that both countries will gain if each produces only the thing it is relatively better at producing and then trades some of what it produces for some of what the other country produces. That's great. In that special case, each country gets more stuff than it would get if it produced both things itself and ignored the benefits of trade.

In the real world, where there are countless products, many countries, and where no one trades stuff for stuff, the theory means nothing. In the real world, where we buy and sell things, it is possible for one country to produce everything, or almost everything, at a lower cost than anyone else.

Even without worrying about that extreme case, the truth is that if the people in your country buy things from other countries, there is no guarantee that anyone in any other country will buy anything from your country.

The even larger truth is that all theories based on assumptions apply only to cases where the assumptions are actually true.

When it comes to foreign trade—which is not trade, but international buying and selling—we have only two hard facts to guide our policies.

One is, as we already know, foreign trade deficits reduce GDP and foreign trade surpluses increase GDP.

The other is that specialization is real. It is not a theory; it is how the world works. As such, specialization is the only logical argument for foreign trade (or commerce). But it is not good enough to let us ignore the importance of trade deficits or surpluses. In other words, specialization is a necessary, but not a sufficient, condition to claim that trade is good.

Just think of what life would be like without specialization; if you couldn't buy anything at all—if you had to be totally self-sufficient; or if you were not allowed to use anything you did not make yourself out of resources you own; or if you couldn't buy anything that wasn't made in the state in which you live, using resources only from your state; or if you couldn't buy anything that wasn't made in America, out of totally American resources. Think of what the country would be like if that were the case for everyone.

That is why, instead of living as self-sufficient farmers, people in free societies choose to get jobs, including jobs as specialized farmers, and to have a good life buying stuff from everywhere.

Of course, the better jobs people have, the better off they are. Think of having a job or a business that makes a good profit selling locally. Then think of what you could make if your product is sold statewide. Then nation wide. Then world wide. Opening up the world gives you higher wages and greater profits.

*That's why free trade is so good.*

Not so fast. It is good. But nothing comes without a cost.

Some say that the only possible "cost" is that some individuals and businesses might suffer in order for the country to benefit, but only temporarily. The argument is that even if imports take away jobs, increased spending will eventually help everyone. The assumption is that even those who lose their jobs or businesses will eventually get new jobs and open new businesses, because if consumers pay lower prices for imported goods, they will have more money to spend on other things.

The problem is that we do not know if the money saved by purchasing cheaper imports will be spent on goods and services produced in the United States. The savings can just as easily be spent on more imports.

So how can we guarantee that jobs and businesses lost to imported goods will be replaced? Or that if they are replaced, wages and profits will be as high as they were before?

We can't. We know that trade agreements that increase exports lead to increases in production, employment, and profits at home. We know that trade agreements that reduce or eliminate restrictions on imports lower prices for consumers. We also know that when we are free to buy and sell things everywhere, individuals and countries gain from specialization.

But those facts do not mean everyone wins. When exports increase, domestic prices can also increase. That was an issue when agricultural exports increased. Farmers liked it. Consumers did not, because food prices increased.

And when imports increase, U.S. production can be hurt. Consumers like it, because they get lower prices. Companies that go out of business, and workers who lose their jobs, do not.

There is one other fact that cannot be ignored. It is: There are no countries with a large and prosperous middle class that do not also have a solid manufacturing base. Countries that earn huge sums of money exporting natural resources, such as oil, have middle class populations only when those in power decide to spread the wealth around, which does happen once in a while.

For all other countries, it is necessary to worry about what "free-trade" agreements do to the manufacturing base. And to the foreign-trade surplus or deficit.

That is why foreign trade is a complex and messy issue with no easy answers, especially the easy, but unfounded, claims that free trade is always good or always bad.

# CHAPTER THIRTY-TWO

# The Federal Reserve

*Is the Federal Reserve really, really smart?*

There are times when the Federal Reserve does a good job; there are other times when the Federal Reserve creates disasters.

*Everyone thinks the Federal Reserve is good.*

It *is* good...*sometimes.* At other times, it is not so good. But because fiscal policy is of limited use, manipulating the money supply *is* the main tool for managing the U.S. economy.

*That's exactly what the Federal Reserve does. So what's wrong?*

To begin with, although the supply of money, or changes in the rate of growth of the money supply, has a dramatic impact on the economy, it was not until 1980 that the money supply in the United States was truly brought under control. But, both before and after 1980, the Federal Reserve was responsible for some of the worst economic times in America.

*Is that your opinion?*

You decide. The Federal Reserve was created in 1913, with the major objective of protecting banks from failure due to large withdrawals. It was to be "the lender of last resort" to banks, thereby preventing bank panics. But, its first big test was the 1920s, and it failed. The fact is that the Federal Reserve had a lot to do with the stock market crash of 1929.

*How?*

The Fed allowed the speculative run-up of stock prices in the 1920s by letting people legally "invest" in stocks by borrowing almost the entire purchase price. Almost anyone could borrow virtually all the money he or she wanted in order to buy stocks. The part *investors* had to put up is called the *margin* or *margin requirement*. If the margin requirement is very low, you can buy stocks with virtually none of your own money.

*Is that bad?*

Not if stock prices always increase, and if the increase is due to real corporate profits. But in the 1920s, prices were rising because of speculative buying, not because of real profits. When it was obvious that the low-margin policy had the stock market running out of control, the Federal Reserve panicked. It raised margin requirements. But when margin requirements increased, "investors" had two choices: They could give more money to their broker or banker to pay for a larger part of the purchases they had already made; or they could sell their stocks. Those who did not have the money needed to hold their stocks were forced to sell. The sell-off of stocks caused prices to fall, and some who held their stocks now owed more than their stocks were worth.

Then, after they sold, they still owed massive amounts of money. That is why, when the market crashed, so many individuals ended up in bankruptcy.

*Then what?*

Then the Federal Reserve allowed banks to fail and the money supply to shrink, which is what it was supposed to prevent from happening. As a result, the Federal Reserve was partly responsible for the length and depth of the Great Depression, because if the Federal Reserve had protected the money supply, the Depression would not have been as severe, and it would probably have been over before World War II ended it. Many blamed the severity of the Depression on bad fiscal policies—the failure of the federal government to use deficit spending to pull the economy out of trouble. But it was really a case of absolutely terrible management of the money supply.

*What else did the Fed do wrong?*

The Federal Reserve was responsible for the inflation of the 1970s, because it kept increasing the money supply to finance the deficit spending on the Vietnam War. And when inflation caused interest rates to rise, the Federal Reserve increased the money supply even more, in an attempt to push rates back down. Interest rates have to rise during inflation, because lenders are not willing to make loans at rates that are less than the inflation rate. If they do, when the loans are repaid, the lender receives money that is worth less, in real purchasing power, than the money it loaned out.

Instead of keeping the money supply under control and letting interest rates rise, which would have choked off the inflation, the Federal Reserve kept increasing the money supply, hoping to keep rates down. But each increase in the money supply added to the rate of inflation. It was a vicious circle that led to the worst modern inflation in the United States.

*What else?*

After deciding to end the inflation of the 1970s by restricting the growth of the money supply, Federal Reserve Chairman Paul Volcker waited almost a year to act, even though there was no reason to let the economy deteriorate for another year. When he did finally reign in the money supply, it was just before the Carter-Reagan election, which meant that the unavoidable and predictable upward explosion of interest rates became an election issue rather than a Federal Reserve issue.

*What else?*

The Federal Reserve was responsible for the stock market crash of 1987, because it raised interest rates to fight what it claimed was the beginning of another inflation. But there was no real threat of inflation, because the only cause of inflation is the Fed itself—when it increases the money supply too fast.

*What else?*

The Federal Reserve was responsible for keeping economic growth below its true potential during the Clinton presidency, because it kept interest rates high to prevent fast economic growth from causing inflation. But fast economic growth does not cause inflation—not in theory and not at any time in history. It was a bogus argument. The Clinton years gave us the longest economic expansion in U.S. history, but the economy could have grown even faster.

*Anything else?*

The Federal Reserve was partly responsible for the recession that began in 2001, because it waited too long to lower interest rates. At the time, the Fed was more concerned with inflation—which was a phony issue—than with recession—which was a real concern—given troubles in the stock market and rising oil prices. By the time the Fed acted, the stock market had crashed, and the economy was in a tailspin.

*Anything else?*

The Federal Reserve played a major role in causing the recession that began in 2008, because it failed to regulate the financial markets it is charged with protecting while, at the same time, encouraging massive corporate gambling on derivatives and credit default swaps. And, as in 2001, the Fed once again believed that the rising oil prices of 2007 were an inflationary, rather than a recessionary, issue. Once again, the Fed was wrong. And once again, the Fed was in the middle of a stock market collapse.

*What do you want to do? Shut down the Fed?*

Not at all. The Federal Reserve, which is the main manager of the American economy, may not have the greatest record. But it is frightening to think of what might happen if politicians took control of the money supply and monetary policy. It would be a massive conflict of interest. Politicians could spend whatever they want, knowing they have the power to create money to finance it. Also, those in control would have the opportunity to disrupt or temporarily improve the economy in order to affect elections.

*But you are saying the Fed has already done that.*

It has. So did the first two central banks in America— the First Bank of the United States and the Second Bank of the United States. Each was shut down after trying to use its power to support a presidential candidate who lost. In each case, the elected president did not renew the bank's charter.

*But the Federal Reserve is different. It was created with all sorts of checks and balances. It lets the government control the money supply without having power concentrated in one place.*

The government does not manage the money supply. The Federal Reserve does. And the Federal Reserve is not a government agency.

*But there are still checks and balances.*

That was the idea when Congress created the Federal Reserve System that began operating in 1913. The President of the United States was given the power to appoint members to the Federal Reserve Board of Governors. The President was also given the power to appoint the Chairman of the Federal Reserve Board. And the Chairman of the Federal Reserve Board is required to testify in front of Congress about Fed policies. But the Federal Reserve System is an independent entity. It is really a central bank that, as in other developed nations, manages the money supply.

*Why is it called the Federal Reserve System?*

On paper, the Federal Reserve is a system, not a single central bank. When Congress created it, it was clear that banks and the money supply had to be managed, especially after the bank panic of 1907 wiped out the savings of so many people. History had proven that banks could not be trusted to regulate themselves. And when banks are out of control, so are the money supply and the economy. But because of the abuses of power by the two former central banks, many in Congress did not want another central bank. The solution, after years of debate, was to create the Federal Reserve System. Rather than having a single central bank, twelve Federal Reserve Banks were established throughout the country. The idea was to spread the power around instead of having it concentrated in one place.

*Has it worked?*

It sounded like a good idea in the beginning, but today it is easy to see that a few individuals—often a single individual—have enormous influence over the economy by being able to control the money supply and interest rates. As I said, the Federal Reserve is not a government agency. It is a central bank with twelve separate Federal Reserve Banks, each of which is owned, through stock purchases, by the commercial banks it is supposed to regulate and supervise. But the New York Federal Reserve Bank handles all the day-to-day operations of the Fed.

*So, you are saying that the U.S. economy is being managed by a bunch of private bankers? People who weren't even elected?*

Not a bunch. A few.

*That's pretty scary. But what is the Federal Reserve supposed to do?*

In the beginning, it's primary function was to be *a lender of last resort* to banks, meaning it would lend funds to banks that could not meet depositor's demands for withdrawals, which meant it was also looking after the money supply. The Federal Reserve did an adequate job for a few years, while the economy was relatively stable. But it did a terrible job of protecting banks, deposits, and the money supply during the Great Depression. Even so, its power and influence grew to the point where it is now the main manager of the U.S. economy, and one of the most powerful economic entities in the world. Today, its stated goals are to achieve acceptable economic growth, low unemployment, and steady prices in the U.S. economy. The tools it has at its disposal are its control of the money supply and the authority to set certain interest rates.

*The textbooks spend a lot of time showing how a multiple expansion or contraction of the money supply can take place in a fractional-reserve banking system. But I don't understand how it works.*

You don't have to understand a fractional-reserve banking system. That's not how the money supply works.

*What do you mean?*

The theory is that when someone makes a deposit in a bank, the bank loans out say 90 percent of the deposit. The loan ends up in another bank that then loans out 90 percent of its deposit. That loan ends up in another bank that then loans out 90 percent of its deposit. And so on. Each deposit and loan in the sequence is smaller, because each is only 90 percent of the previous deposit. And all the loans that end up in checking accounts are counted as money. Therefore, in theory, the whole process leads to an expansion of the money supply that can be as much as ten times the original deposit. The greater the fraction of each deposit that banks can legally loan out, the greater is the increase in the money supply. The percentage of deposits that must be held as legal reserves—and not loaned out— is called the reserve requirement. The Federal Reserve sets the legal reserve requirement, so, in theory, the Fed can increase the money supply by lowering the reserve requirement, thereby allowing banks to make more loans.

*But you said it doesn't work.*

Not like that. There are too many *leakages* in the process to get a large multiple of the money supply. All the loans do not go into banks or checking accounts. That's why the Federal Reserve's true method for increasing or decreasing the money supply is its Open Market Operations.

*So what do I have to know?*

All you have to know is that when the Fed wants to increase the money supply, it simply buys government bonds in the bond market. When the Fed buys bonds, it replaces something that is not money—bonds—with something that is money—Federal Reserve checks. If the Fed wants to decrease the money supply, it sells government securities in the bond market. When the Fed sells bonds, it replaces something that is money—checks drawn against deposits in banks—with something that is not money—bonds. In reality, the increase or decrease in the money supply is, for all practical purposes, equal to the Fed's purchase or sale of bonds.

*That's it?*

That's it. But, as simple as the open market process is, it is the most powerful tool available for managing modern economies.

*Who decides to increase or decrease the money supply, or to change the rate of growth of the money supply?*

Technically, the Federal Open Market Committee makes the decision.

*What's that?*

The Federal Open Market Committee consists of the seven members of the Federal Reserve Board of Governors and five of the twelve Federal Reserve Bank presidents. Four of the five individual bank presidents are selected on a rotating basis. The president of the Federal Reserve Bank of New York is always on the committee, because the Fed's open market operations are conducted through the New York Bank.

*What is* the Board of Governors?

The Board of Governors is seven people appointed by the President of the United States to staggered 14-year terms that end in January of every even numbered year. The president also appoints the Chairman of the Board of Governors to a four-year term that is staggered with the president's, so that when a president takes office, it is with an existing Chairman. The idea was to prevent any president from easily taking over the Board with his own appointees. The presidents of the twelve regional Federal Reserve Banks are appointed by each bank's nine directors, six of whom are chosen by the member banks in the district.

*Pretty complicated.*

It is. It was developed by Congress to prevent the concentration of power in one place. But, as I said, today's reality is that power is not only centered in one place, it is centered with one person: the Chairman of the Federal Reserve Board of Governors.

*But monetary policy can still be used to regulate or manage the economy?*

Within limits. A policy that has the money supply growing too fast causes inflation. And there are questions regarding the ability of monetary policy to pull an economy out of a deep recession. In the 1930s, Keynes argued that there was a natural rate of interest—a level below which interest rates would not fall. If true, it meant that monetary policy, based on lowering interest rates to encourage spending and business investment, was limited. According to the theory, once the bottom was reached for interest rates, additional increases in the money supply would do nothing to increase economic activity because interest rates could not be forced any lower.

*Was Keynes right?*

No. We know—logically and historically—that interest rates can fall to zero. Adjusted for inflation, the real rate of interest can even be negative.

*If that's true, why is monetary policy limited in what it can do?*

Because disproving the downward limit on interest rates does not automatically prove the value of monetary policy.

*What do you mean?*

It is true that as interest rates fall, business and consumer spending increases. The lower the rate of interest, the smaller the payments on loans will be. But there will still be payments, because the loans still have to be paid off. Even if interest rates drop to zero, the money has to be paid back. Zero interest does not mean free money; it means there is no cost to borrow money. And the ability to pay back a loan depends on future income. A business cannot borrow money to fund expenditures it does not expect to recover, even at a zero rate of interest. An individual will not buy a car, even at a zero rate of interest, without considering the future payments and alternative uses of future income.

That is why pushing interest rates to zero in Japan was not enough to pull the Japanese economy out of a recession. And why everyone does not run out and buy a new car at a zero rate of interest.

The deeper a recession becomes, the less important additional declines in interest rates are to people and businesses making decisions about borrowing money to make purchases or investments, partly because interest rates are already very low. But also because even a zero rate of interest may not be enough to allow firms with poor prospects or individuals without jobs to make purchases on credit.

*That is why there are limits to what monetary policy can do?*

That's it. However, that does not negate the overall value and importance of monetary policy. What it does do is give us one more reason for avoiding the mistakes that cause recessions.

*So, what should we do?*

We should be more watchful over what the Federal Reserve is doing. If the Federal Reserve is the main manager of the U.S. economy, it should be more answerable for its policies and actions. There should be more debate in Congress about the assumptions the Fed is making about the economy and about what its policies should be.

A good place to begin is to make it clear that the textbooks, and the Fed, are wrong when they offer two explanations for inflation: demand pull and cost-push. The truth is, there is no such thing as cost-push inflation, which is why it is always wrong to use the term "stagflation" to describe an economy that is both stagnant and suffering from inflation.

To be accurate, there is only one cause of inflation: demand pull, meaning that excessive demand pulls prices higher.

But there are two types of recession: cost push recession and falling demand recession. If everyone understood that an increase in the Consumer Price Index caused by rising oil prices is a signal of a possible recession, not inflation, we, meaning the Fed, would not make so many mistakes.

# CHAPTER THIRTY-THREE

# Rubber Ducky Economics: A Summary

*Someone asked the speaker if he could summarize the meeting. His answer was that he could do better than that. He said he had prepared a short, written summary of the main points and that he would now hand it out. He explained that he did not want to hand it out at the beginning of the meeting, because he wanted everyone to listen rather than read.*

### Rubber Ducky Economics: A Summary

We use a bathtub to represent the economy.

The water in the tub represents Gross Domestic Product.

The water flowing in is:
>consumer spending,
>investment spending,
>government spending, and
>exports.

The water flowing out is:
>imports.

And we need just the right amount of money in the economy.
>Too much money and we get inflation.
>Too little money and we can have a recession.

The actual quantity of water in the tub, after some given time period, depends on how much is coming in and how much is going out.

We decide if the quantity of water in the tub is acceptable by tracking unemployment and growth numbers and the rate of inflation.

If we do not like the quantity of water in the tub, we can look at ways to change the inflow or the outflow.

There are a number of ways to change the inflow or outflow.

Fiscal policy—meaning changes in taxes or government spending intended to improve the overall economy—may not work; or if it does, it may have a minimal impact, other than a redistribution of income.

Monetary policy—meaning changing the money supply (or the rate of increase of the money supply) to improve the overall economy—does work, because we know that changing interest rates changes consumer spending and investment spending by business. On the other hand, if the Federal Reserve mismanages the money supply, it can cause either inflation or recession. The Federal Reserve can also affect interest rates directly by changing the discount rate, which is the rate of interest the Fed charges banks that borrow money from the Fed to meet the legal reserve requirements set by the Fed.

Correcting the misallocation of resources caused by market failures, public goods, positive externalities, negative externalities, and common property resources, increases economic efficiency, which increases real income, consumption, and GDP. Foreign trade agreements that increase exports relative to imports add directly to GDP.

# CHAPTER THIRTY-FOUR

# I Knew That

As the crowd was leaving the park, David Peterson, Brenda Jones, and Kevin and Karen Elmwood approached the bandstand together. All were thinking, *I knew that.* But all had the same question. Brenda Jones was the first to speak.

"Thank you," she said to the speaker, "If this had been the opening lecture for any of the economics courses I took in college, we could have spent an entire semester reading about and discussing the real world instead of spending most of our time on dead theories. I do have one question. How does your bathtub model fit with politics? Is it liberal? Or conservative?"

The man standing beside the bathtub smiled. "In the first place," he said, "it's not my bathtub model. It's yours. It is yours to use and to share. In the second place, people choose political parties for many reasons. And, after joining that party and choosing to believe in the principles or doctrine of that party, they tend to vote for that party's candidates. That is what democracy is about—diversity of opinion. But, in an ideal world, individual opinions and the doctrine of political parties would be based on knowledge and facts, not fear and personal bias."

"But, if everyone understood what you said today, wouldn't everyone join the same political party?" Karen asked.

"Not at all," the economist said. "Whether it is economics or physics, people who understand their field can still disagree. They seldom disagree about the basic principles and theories that are the foundation of their discipline. But they often disagree on how those principles apply to the real world. When it comes to voting, many things go into each person's decision.

And, although we believe in the freedom that comes from fair democratic votes, when it comes to understanding how the economy can affect your business, your investments, or your life, I recommend that you rely on economic facts, not political doctrine."

# CHAPTER THIRTY-FIVE

# A Few Facts to Remember

*Someone else asked the speaker if he could offer a few conclusions. He did. In fact, he had another handout prepared. At the top of the handout, he had written:*

**If everyone understood the following short list of economic facts, the world could change overnight**.

*Rising oil prices do not cause inflation.*
Rising oil prices lead to increases in the Consumer Price Index. But all increases in the Consumer Price Index are not a signal of inflation. Sometimes, an increase in the CPI signals a recession, which is the case when oil prices increase.

*There is no such thing as stagflation.*
The term stagflation was meant to describe an economy suffering from stagnation and inflation at the same time, but that is impossible. An economic slowdown caused by rising oil prices should be called a "cost-push recession."

*The only real cause of inflation is too much money.*
The only cause of inflation is having too much money in the economy. Therefore, in the United States, only the Federal Reserve can cause inflation. But it does not have to be too much paper money. When Spain sent ships to the new world, they came back loaded with gold. And that gold, which was money, caused the inflation that helped bring down the Spanish Empire.

*Controlling the money supply controls inflation.*
If the only cause of inflation is too much money, then the cure for inflation is simply to control the money supply.

*The Federal Reserve controls the money supply.*
It does so through its open market operations—buying and selling government bonds in the open market.

*There are many possible causes for recession.*
There are two different kinds of recession: insufficient-demand recession (caused by the bursting of a speculative bubble, a large decrease in the money supply, or something that reduces production, employment, wages, and profits) and cost-push recession (caused by rising resource costs). The Great Depression began with the bursting of a speculative stock-market bubble, and the Federal Reserve turned it into a depression by allowing banks to fail, by letting the money supply implode, and by not protecting individual deposits in banks. The recession that began in 2007 started with a massive increase in oil prices in the summer of 2007 and became a deep recession when the speculative bubble tied to mortgages, derivatives, and credit-default swaps burst. Once again, as in the 1920s, the root cause was a lack of regulation on highly-leveraged "investments."

*The national debt is a problem in a global economy.*
National debt in a global economy is different from national debt when the debt is held domestically. If paying interest on and redeeming government bonds, which are the national debt, means sending money to foreigners, the negative impact of a large national debt can severely affect the future economy.

*There is no natural business cycle.*
That does not mean people will stop looking for one.

*Macroeconomic policies intended to bring an economy out of a recession (meaning changes in taxes or government spending, or changes in the money supply and interest rates) are of questionable value.*

The theoretical predictions of an increase in GDP due to tax cuts or increased government spending (fiscal policy) or increases in the money and decreases in interest rates (monetary policy) must be weighed against the fact that negative "side effects" offset the expected benefits.

*Microeconomic government policies, meaning regulations that protect markets and unowned resources as well as the production of public goods, increase GDP.*

Economists assume that buyers and sellers are driven by greed (even if they are nice people), and that competitive markets turn that greed into individual happiness, profits for business, and an increase in the common good. However, it is only when markets are perfectly competitive that economists claim that government interference is unnecessary or that government interference might reduce economic efficiency. In theory, a perfectly competitive market is self-regulating. But perfectly competitive markets do not exist in the real world, which is why government regulation is a necessary part of a private enterprise economy.

*Correcting market failure increases GDP.*

Monopoly power can reduce economic efficiency and GDP. Government policies that correct the inefficiency increase GDP.

*Correcting negative externalities increases GDP.*

Pollution reduces economic efficiency and GDP. Government policies that correct the inefficiency due to negative neighborhood effects increase GDP.

*Correcting positive externalities increases GDP.*
If government fails to deal with positive externalities, such as education, economic efficiency and GDP are reduced.

*Providing public goods increases GDP.*
If government fails to provide public goods, such as national defense, economic efficiency and GDP are reduced.

*Managing common property resources increases GDP.*
Failing to manage unowned resources, such as fish in lakes and oceans, reduces economic efficiency and GDP.

*Managing foreign trade increases GDP.*
Specialization in production, which is the main benefit of foreign trade, adds to GDP. A foreign trade surplus also adds to GDP. But a foreign trade deficit subtracts from GDP. Therefore, in order for "free trade" to increase GDP, trade must be managed so that the benefits from specialization and exports are not more than offset by a foreign trade deficit. Whether or not that happens is a question of fact, not theory.

# Commonly Used Terms

**Cartel**: An organization of producers that colludes in order to control a market. OPEC is an example. It is a reason for market failure that can lead to a restriction of output and an increase in prices.

**Common Property Resources**: Resources not owned by anyone until someone takes them. It is a cause of market failure that destroys economic efficiency. It can be corrected only by government actions.

**Consumer Price Index**: The Consumer Price Index calculates the cost of a given "basket" of goods for different time periods. The measure assigns weights to items based on the percentage of total expenditures they accounted for during a base period.

**Debt**, **Federal Government**: Outstanding bonds sold by the government to cover past annual deficits.

**Deficit**: An annual shortfall between government revenues and expenditures. Can be financed by selling bonds, raising taxes, or by cutting government spending.

**Demand, market**: The maximum quantity of a good or service buyers are willing and able to buy during a given time period at various prices.

**Discount Rate**: The rate of interest The Federal Reserve charges banks that borrow money from the Fed to meet legal reserve requirements. This is one of the interest rates the media likes to watch, because when the Fed changes the discount rate, other interest rates tend to follow.

**Efficiency**: Economic efficiency means resources are used in ways that maximize the satisfaction of society.

**Equilibrium**: A market equilibrium occurs when there is a price at which the quantity buyers are willing and able to buy is equal to the quantity sellers are willing and able to sell.

**Federal Funds Rate**: The rate of interest banks charge each other when they borrow money from each other to meet the legal reserve requirements set by the Federal Reserve.

**Federal Reserve**: The central bank of the U.S. It regulates commercial banks, controls the money supply, and conducts monetary policy to alter economic performance.

**Fiscal Policy**: Changing taxes and/or government spending to improve the economy. It does not work very well, unless the Federal Reserve finances the deficit by creating money.

**Imperfect Competition**: A market where a buyer or seller affects price. Includes monopoly and monopolistic competition. It is an example of market failure.

**Inflation**: Constantly rising prices over time. It means the purchasing power of money is declining. It is caused when too much money is put into the economy.

**Interest Rates**: A general equilibrium variable that is the cost of borrowing money. The Federal Reserve can control interest rates by controlling the supply of money and by setting some interest rates.

**Market Failure**: A technical term meaning that prices do not allocate resources efficiently. Can be caused by imperfect competition, such as monopoly, or externalities.

**Monetary Policy**: Changing the money supply to affect interest rates and the economy. It is the most effective tool for managing the economy.

**Money supply**: The most used designations are M1 and M2. M1 is defined as coins and currency in circulation plus deposits in checking accounts. M2 is M1 plus savings accounts, money market accounts, and CDs of less than $100,000. Coins are produced by the U.S. Mint. Paper money is printed for the Federal Reserve by the Bureau of Printing & Engraving.

**Monopolistic Competition**: An industry with a small number of large firms, where each producer has an identifiable product, most often with a brand name. It is the main form of business in America.

**Monopoly**: Market failure that occurs when a single firm controls an industry.

**Negative externalities**: Harmful byproducts of production or consumption that are external to the producer or consumer, such as pollution. An example of market failure that reduces economic efficiency.

**Oligopoly**: A market with a small number of producers. It is one type of imperfect competition that causes market failure.

**Perfect Competition**: A theoretical concept. A market where no firm or individual is large enough to affect price. It assumes that the products of each producer in a market are identical, and that competition is the result of producers trying to produce at the lowest cost.

**Positive externalities**: A positive byproduct of production or consumption that is external to the producer or consumer. Education is an example. Without government help, the free market will not provide a sufficient quantity of goods with positive externalities to maximize the wealth of the nation.

**Producer Price Index**: The PPI, from the Bureau of Labor Statistics, is used to measure average price changes received by domestic producers. Began in 1891 when the U.S. Senate authorized the Senate Committee on Finance to estimate the impact of tariffs on exports and imports, growth, and prices in both agriculture and manufacturing. Was called the Wholesale Price Index until 1978.

**Public goods**: Goods and services whose benefits cannot be excluded from those who do not pay for them. In almost all cases, such goods can be provided only by government.

**Recession**: An economic slowdown with rising unemployment and little or no economic growth. A depression is a severe recession.

**Reserve Requirements**: The percentage of deposits banks are required to hold as reserves against potential withdrawals. Set by The Fed.

**Supply, market**: The maximum quantity of a good or service sellers are willing and able to sell during a given time period at various prices.

**Wealth**: The nation's *real* wealth takes account not only of money or financial wealth, but also the environment and things such as economic stability, crime, and health, that add to or take away from the well-being of society and of individuals.

# Author's Conclusion

Freedom is about conquering fear, which is why slave owners prevented slaves from learning to read and write. They knew that literacy leads to asking questions, which leads to knowledge, which overcomes fear, which then leads to a demand for freedom. It is also why dictators are quick to burn books and take control of education.

If you cannot read and write, you are at the mercy of others. You have to trust someone else to tell you what has been written and what you are signing, which means living in fear.

Being economically literate is the same. If you have just a little knowledge of the economy, you do not have to lay awake at night, fearing what others are telling you about the inflation, recession, or depression they claim is descending upon you, likening each new disaster to a plague sprinkled on the undeserving by God Himself.

In the end, economic literacy, like language literacy, is about power. Throughout history, the easiest way for those in power to maintain control has been to keep the people illiterate. It is the same with economics. Because of the importance of the economy in everyone's life, and because of the fear that can be fostered by predicting economic disruptions or disasters, the only way to be truly free is to understand just a little bit about real—meaning non-partisan—economics.

Over the years, I have listened to countless successful businesspeople, people who run the largest corporations in America, talk about the world. Almost without exception, some topic would come up and he or she would say, "Well, I really don't understand economics." Or, "That's probably better left to economists."

Why? Why would some of the world's smartest and most successful people say they do not understand economics?

The answer is simple. The reason economics does not make sense to many people is not because those people cannot understand logical arguments, but because there are too many illogical arguments in economics.

The thing economists have done best is to convince almost everyone that economics is not only extremely difficult, but that many of its theoretical conclusions are "counterintuitive."

What does it mean to be counterintuitive? Economists like to think it means that economic knowledge is superior to "uneducated expectations."

Unfortunately, the counterintuitive idea has led economists to accept conclusions that contradict reason, knowledge, and facts, not just blind expectations or intuition. Which may be why many economic arguments do not make sense to rational and logical individuals. Which is why I wrote this little book.

At its core, the economy is easy to understand. The only things that are difficult to understand are the elegant mathematical theories that are either illogical or based on unrealistic or knowingly false assumptions. And because illogical arguments have little value in the real world, I left them out.